Harvey W. Seeds American Legion Post #29 History

RALPH A. MORALES

Copyright © 2018 Ralph A Morales

All rights reserved. No part of this book may be reproduced or transmitted in any form or by any means, electronic or mechanical, including photocopying, recording, or by any information storage and retrieval system without the written permission of the author, except where permitted by law.

ISBN-10:0692128492
ISBN-13: 978-0-692-12849-7

DEDICATION

To my beautiful wife, Debora, who, like many military wives, didn't realize what I signed us up for when I re-enlisted or when I took on this project, but supported me regardless.

HARVEY W. SEEDS

AMERICAN LEGION PREAMBLE

For God and country we associate ourselves together for the following purposes:

To uphold and defend the Constitution of the United States of America;

To maintain law and order;

To foster and perpetuate a one hundred percent Americanism;

To preserve the memories and incidents of our associations in the Great Wars;

To inculcate a sense of individual obligation to the community, state and nation;

To combat the autocracy of both the classes and the masses;

To make right the master of might;

To promote peace and goodwill on earth;

To safeguard and transmit to posterity the principles of justice, freedom and democracy;

To consecrate and sanctify our comradeship by our devotion to mutual helpfulness

CONTENTS

PREFACE	VI	SPIRIT OF '76	117
ACKNOWLEDGMENTS	VIII	RUSSIANS	122
TIMELINE	XI	BLIGHT	127
MIAMI: A CONDENSED HISTORY	14	END OF AN ERA	136
PROLOGUE	19	FOUR PILLARS	139
BIRTH OF THE LEGION	22	HISTORICAL PROGRAMS	142
HARVEY W. SEEDS	26	PAST COMMANDERS	147
FOUNDING FATHERS	31	AUXILIARY	173
THE BIG BLOW	42	40 & 8	176
SECOND AEF	48	BASEBALL	178
THE DEPRESSION	53	DRUM CORPS	181
THE DRUMS OF WAR	71	COLOR GUARD	192
VETERAN'S VILLAGE	85	GUARD OF HONOR	194
BLACK VETERANS	88	YOUR MEMBERSHIP CARD	197
OLD TIMERS	91	POST #29 EVERLASTING	198
KOREA	96	CURRENT COMMANDER	206
AMERICANISM	101	WORKS CITED	207
VIETNAM	106	INDEX	211

PREFACE

The first time I saw the Harvey W. Seeds archives I was at once excited and appalled. Many of the documents I found in bankers boxes or old file cabinets, in rooms the Legion could not afford to cool properly, never mind monitor for mildew or other deteriorating factors. More than a few priceless photos were insect-eaten, mildewed, or faded beyond repair. A couple crumbled in my hands as I opened them for the first time in many years. When I wrapped my head around what I was seeing, I realized how much of the material we have lost to time.

This organization, the American Legion, just like a military or government department, was fastidious about creating documents regarding almost all of their actions or transactions. On occasion some of the bookkeeping was less comprehensive than during other periods. At some point in time between 1949 and 1952, an effort was made to either clean up or scrap some 'old,' papers and many of the day-to-day documents that existed were destroyed.

This post has dwindled to just a few people in positions of leadership a number of times in its history. Some years there were no Adjutants or Historians or Chaplains, or enough people in the Executive Committee to run a proper meeting, much less take notes and keep records.

The keepers of our documents didn't protect the papers as a properly trained librarian or historian would, but they did something more important. They kept the torch lit on the precepts of the Legion, never quitting on an organization that had neglected some of them early on.

They passed on the indelible, inextinguishable flame of our shared history.

Struggling to maintain this narrative in a chronological format, I took some editorial liberties to make the story flow for the reader. The dedicated Appendices to the Auxiliary, 40 & 8, drum corps and programs serve the content better and do not leave it sprinkled throughout the hundred years of our story.

Photographs are all from Harvey Seeds archives and from Bob Zinko. Wherever applicable, I left the scribbled names and notes on them.

The words Veteran and Soldier are always capitalized in my texts, as is the Army style, a symbol of respect., "lest we forget."

ACKNOWLEDGMENTS

Many stories were left untold in this endeavor. I have not had the luxury of taking this task on full-time. This yearbook was developed to commemorate 100 years of Legion activity in Miami and the deadline wasn't going to budge. I regret being unable to reconstruct the histories of the Auxiliary, the *Sons of the American Legion* and the *40 & 8* in any detail. Perhaps the next edition will allow me more time to study them. I am sure there were at least a hundred more men and women I should have recognized or mentioned. I couldn't go down every rabbit hole and investigate every lead. The fact that there are so many great stories just within our post membership is a testament to the idea of a *Greatest Generation*. There is, however, more than one great generation and there were and still are so many patriots.

Post Historian is a lonely position. The people who talk to me most are long gone to their reward.

I have to thank Arthur Keene (Historian 1920-1923, *40 & 8* and Department Historian), Herbert U. Feibelman (Post Historian 1941-1953,1954-1959), Joe Frank (Past Commander and Cracker Legionnaire Editor), P/C J.K. Williams and past historians John B Williams, Cameron Craig and Georgia Lyons. Without their work, this project could not have taken its form and volume. Lyons put together a formidable award-winning yearbook in 1978 that can be considered the standard by which others should be measured. She even took most of the photographs in the book herself. Williams wrote *The Williams Chronicle*, a whimsical description of each Past Commander as he remembered them, which helped me meet them through his eyes.

Comrade Feibelman's greatest legacy as Post Historian is unequivocally his 1960 book, *History of Harvey W. Seeds Post No. 29 American Legion,* published in 1960. Without him and that book, I would have been lost. He was my compass and I kept referring to his work throughout my own for nuggets of information that would corroborate what I'd found elsewhere or to turn me onto other interesting subjects.

I can't imagine what his research days must have been like, with no computer and a full-time job as an attorney. As he said, "This voluntary contribution to the record … merely hits the high spots…and can overlook some. Zealous effort is still subject to human frailty." [1]

Dawn Hughes of the Miami History museum, *History Miami* is, to me, our most important librarian in Miami right now. She is a keeper of knowledge I hope that organization is working on preserving. She not only knows the subject matter, but she knows people and in this era of a million electronic dead-ends, she is always helpful with a way forward, a kind word, or even a phone number from her Rolodex.

Jean McNamee, daughter of the late, great Cesar La Monaca was a touchstone to the past. She brought the faded print, the grainy videos and black and white photos to life for me and inspired me to continue telling these stories.

A final acknowledgement and a million *thank-you's* must go to the hundreds of beat writers, editors and staff at the Miami News, Miami Herald, Miami Metropolis, Biscayne Boulevard Times and

---

[1] Herbert Feibelman, *History of Harvey W. Seeds..* (Miami, Review Print, 1960), Introduction

the other publications that printed the stories of these lives. Their countless hours of aggregating names and journaling the American experience paid off not only by filling newspaper column inches but in preserving the rich history our forefathers created.

Without writers, without newspapers and journals transferring the knowledge and truth of our accomplishments , our culture is diminished.

TIMELINE

January 1909: Union Veterans form an association that meets the first Monday of each month in Miami

July 2, 1913: Over 50,000 Civil War veterans reunite at Gettysburg

July 28, 1914: Austria-Hungary declares war on Serbia. World War I begins

April 6, 1917: The United States declares war on Germany

May 1917: The Selective Service Act, *the draft*, is enacted. Eventually 2.8 million American men are drafted

October 21, 1917: The first U.S. Soldiers enter combat in France

July 16, 1918: Harvey W. Seeds becomes the first Dade County resident killed in action in World War I

November 11, 1918: World War I ends, officially

March 1919: The American Legion is born at the Paris Caucus, Paris, France

April 10, 1919: William P Smith, Mayor of Miami calls for the first meeting of Miami Veterans of WWI

May 8-10, 1919: The St Louis Caucus of the national American Legion gives rise to the Legion preamble, elected leaders and the founding convention site, Minneapolis

June 10-11, 1919: The first Florida Department convention is held in Jacksonville, Florida. 24 posts apply for charters. Albert H. Blanding is elected the first Department Commander

August 6, 1919: Harvey W. Seeds, American Legion Post #29 of Florida, applies for its charter

September 16, 1919: Congress adopts and allows the national incorporation of the American Legion

November 11, 1919: Four Legionnaires are killed as they confront IWW, union members in Centralia, Washington

October 22-25, 1934: American Legion's sixteenth annual convention is held in Miami, Florida

September 1, 1939: WWII begins as Nazi Germany invades Poland

June 22, 1944: The Serviceman's Readjustment Act, G.I. Bill is signed into law by President Roosevelt

September 2, 1945: Japan formally surrenders and WWII ends

October 8-21, 1948: American Legion's thirtieth annual convention is held in Miami, Florida

June 25, 1950: The Korean War begins as North Korean troops enter South Korea

October 15-18, 1951: American Legion's thirty-third annual convention is held in Miami, Florida

July 27, 1953: Armistice signing brings a cessation of hostilities but no treaty to end the Korean conflict

October 10-13, 1955: American Legion's thirty-seventh annual convention is held in Miami, Florida

November 1, 1955: The U.S. begins sending military advisors to Vietnam

October 15-20, 1960: American Legion's forty second annual convention is held in Miami Beach, Florida

September 6-12, 1963: American Legion's forty fifth annual convention is held in Miami Beach, Florida

August 16-22, 1974: American Legion's fifty-sixth annual convention is held in Miami Beach, Florida

April 30, 1975: The last U.S. Marines leave the U.S. embassy in Saigon, Vietnam

August 2, 1990: Iraq annexes and invades Kuwait. Operation Desert Shield is initiated and American troops move into the area

February 28, 1991: President Bush declares a cease fire, declares Kuwait freed and begins to withdraw troops from the Middle East

September 11, 2001: Coordinated terror attacks kill 2,996 people using hijacked civilian aircraft.

October 7, 2001: Following the 9/11 attacks, the U.S. invades Afghanistan after the country's government refuses to cooperate in handing over terrorists affiliated with the 9/11 attacks.

March 20, 2003: The U.S. invades Iraq after accusing Saddam Hussein of having weapons of mass destruction.

December 18, 2011: The U.S. withdraws the last of its fighting forces from Iraq.

In 2018, America's involvement in Afghanistan will eclipse all the time Americans were on the ground in Vietnam and become the longest military conflict in American history.

MIAMI – A CONDENSED HISTORY

From the beginning, Miami's history has been tied to the military.

First explored by the Spaniards, Florida changed flags a number of times from the moment it was discovered, to the moment it became a state in 1845. It was a place for many 'firsts,' but some are overlooked because American history, as we have read it in schools, is usually written from a white Anglo-centric point of view.

The first muster of a militia in the Americas was conducted by the Spanish in 1565 in St. Augustine, Florida, decades before the Mayflower landed, a fact unpopular in Massachusetts, but one the Florida National Guard embraces as its legacy.

Florida's rich Native American history is fundamental to why, when and how Miami was developed.

Fort Dallas was built at the mouth of the Miami River in 1836 by the US Army in an attempt to quell South Florida's indigenous Native American population, collectively referred to as *Seminoles* during the *Second Seminole War*. They were what we now know as Miccosukee.

Before then, very few settlers wanted to remain in what was basically swampy marshes replete with native pine, palms, snakes and alligators.

On July 28, 1896 just a few months after developer, Henry Flagler's railroad arrived, the city was incorporated.

The Spanish-American War in 1898, made Miami America's gateway to the south. The taking-over by the United States of Puerto Rico and (temporarily) Cuba was to mean a much wider

American appreciation of the Caribbean region.

"Everglades Reclamation," what we now understand as a massive error in developmental arrogance, started in 1906. The State dredged canals and sold great tracts of land to housing companies. Sellers promoted the joy of owning a little piece of fabulously rich soil in a land of warmth and sunshine. Developers cut into millions of acres of natural habitat, drained it for commercial and residential use and created the myriad of ecological issues we have inherited going into the next century.

Miami Beach was incorporated as a town in 1915 but for years the area was a sleepy backwater visited by the rich and only for winter vacations.

It wasn't until World War I, when aviation was born, that South Florida really boomed. The fact that early flyers depended on good weather (visual flight rules), thrust the area into international attention. South Florida is one of the few places on the American east coast that doesn't have to deal with fog or many clouds on a regular basis. Five of 35 U.S. military flight schools in 1918 were built in Florida.

Through 1925, it was becoming *Greater Miami* with a vengeance. Real estate was incredibly active and property sales fed almost every other sector of the economy. A growing community needed more land and houses, more stores and churches, larger theatres and other buildings. More houses for sale meant more ads in the newspaper, more construction jobs, more police jobs and so on.

The upswing continued until the Great Miami Hurricane of 1926. The storm brought construction and real estate sales to a grinding halt.

Conditions in the Miami area were just beginning to improve, with the help of Post #29, when news came of the Wall Street crash. It was the beginning of the worst economic period in the modern history of the United States, the *Great Depression*.

Miami weathered *The Depression*, some would say, better than a lot of the country.

With world-wide social and economic conditions in decline, the stage was set for Word War II. Although no major battles were fought in the Caribbean, Florida in general and Miami specifically were of vital geo-strategic importance. As America beefed up its military in the Sunshine state, it developed a generation of Veterans that learned to appreciate the sometimes brutal climate.

After World War II, millions of people (a lot of them Veterans) flocked to Florida. The state's economy boomed again.

Organized criminals considered the area a neutral territory where no major business was transacted, so while there were plenty of vice-type crimes, illegal gambling, prostitution, the violence seen in similarly-sized metro areas did not occur in Miami. It was mid-century tropical- idyllic for many.

January 1, 1959 marked Fidel Castro's, " revolutionary victory," in Cuba. He marched into Havana that day and over 100,000 Cubans quickly fled to the U.S. as political refugees. This fundamentally changed the future of the city of Miami.

Miami wasn't central to the *Civil Rights Movement* or protests that rocked the country in the 60's and 70's but it did have its own problems which boiled over, like they do everywhere else.

From 1974 through 1975, 20 bombs exploded in Miami. Most of

them were set by fervent anti-Communists, targeting Dominican or Bahamian interests or anyone who the perpetrators though sympathized with Cuban dictator, Fidel Castro. A few, including one that killed anti-Communist Rolando Masferrer, seemed to be set by Communists or sympathizers in response.

1980 was a period of intense upheaval. Arthur McDuffie, a black motorcyclist was beaten to death by police officers, who were later acquitted of criminal responsibility. 150,000 more Cuban refugees fled Cuba and headed to Miami in the *Mariel Boatlift*. The year culminated in a race riot where thousands of young blacks looted, vandalized and some attacked police. Nineteen people were killed. Hundreds were arrested. Over 3900 Florida National Guard Soldiers were activated.

The city saw a resurgence in popular culture in the 80's as the TV show, *Miami Vice* became a household name, shining a light on the area, warts-and-all, as Miami had become the epicenter for drug smuggling from the Caribbean and South America. Violent crimes grew in number and ferocity.

The next thirty years saw steady growth in real estate but really in all sectors and Miami developed into a mature metropolis. The arts grew up: The ballet was born, local and regional orchestras and symphonies came into existence, foodies from all over the globe opened restaurants. Professional sports teams brought franchises to town. The foundation of a vibrant, multi-cultural city was poured.

The great recession of 2008 hurt South Florida as the area has remained historically sensitive to real estate prices. Luxury condominiums, second-homes, and vacation homes account for thousands of sales annually, bringing millions of dollars in real estate commissions and tax dollars to the local economy.

After a number of booms and busts, Miami is again America's vibrant gateway to the Caribbean and Latin America and is itself a destination for many who don't want to venture farther afield.

It looks like Miami is again in a boom.

PROLOGUE

On March 19 1917, as tensions escalated in Europe, Miami hotelier and businessman Charles Mills volunteered for service in the U.S. Navy.

Dr. E.K. Jaudon was tasked as member of the Miami draft board. As one of the few doctors in the area, he was in charge of conducting physicals for potential Soldiers, a job he could have kept for the duration of the war. Instead, he applied for a commission in the Army and found himself in a Captain's uniform a few months later.

Lydia Marie Christiansen and Alice Flory Coursen, members of Miami pioneer families in an age when women could not yet vote, enlisted in the military.

On April 6, Simon Pierre Robineau picked up his newspaper and found that the U.S. Congress had voted for entering World War I. Robineau had been married less than a year. He had recently moved to Miami and was a partner in a successful law firm with his name on the marquis, *Rose and Robineau*. At that moment, however, he decided that he was getting back into what could now be called *The Great War*.

He spoke to his law partner and went home to discuss his plans with his new wife. Many Americans had already done the same, but this would be Robineau's second enlistment in the same war. By the end of the year, he was in Europe.

Robineau was a US citizen when he volunteered for the French Army in 1914. His parents brought him to America as a boy and he attended middle and high school near Chicago. Born in Versailles, France, he kept a promise he had made to his father, to help his native country should France ever find herself in need.

In 1917, France was in need of all the help she could get.

Robineau was not the young, tall doughboy, featured in ads, that the Allies hoped America would send to Europe to help end the war. He was nearing 30. He had been discharged from the French Army with what were considered near-fatal wounds and had moved to Miami to recuperate. He wore round spectacles, as were fashionable at the time. One account says he had a slight limp.

Whatever his physical imperfections, soon Robineau found himself in Europe in an American uniform. He was in charge of over 200 *interpreters*. He travelled the battlefield as a liaison between the allied armies. *Interpreter* was a euphemism for clandestine operator, spy. Robineau, himself, spoke at least three languages and helped manage intelligence operations for the U.S. Army.

His actions on the battlefield earned him an American *Purple Heart* and the French *Ordre de l'Etoile Noir* (Chevalier) by presidential decree, among other awards.

Robineau returned to Miami after the war and re-joined his law practice, he was an early member of the American Legion, ran for and won election to multiple elected offices at the city and state level. He had a successful civilian life, until history intervened, again.

If two combat tours were somehow not selfless enough, Robineau, facing age 50, donned the uniform once more during World War II and was promoted to Colonel, Army Air Corps, as he resumed intelligence duties focusing on occupied France.

Within our post's membership there are a hundred stories of

battlefield bravado, countless medals and accolades; men and women who did whatever the country asked.

More than a few made the ultimate sacrifice.

It is that unquantifiable spirit, the idealism of selfless service that is the highest precept of the American Legionnaire and the American serviceman and servicewoman, that makes up the soul of this organization.

BIRTH OF THE LEGION

James K Williams was born in Georgia and moved to Florida as a child. In 1917 he enlisted in the Florida National Guard in Miami's Company M, which saw fit to send him back to Georgia for basic training. Within a year he commissioned as a lieutenant and the Guard was federalized. He was attached to the 38th Infantry Division. Deployed near the end of the war, he didn't see much *action*, however, he found himself in Paris in March of 1919 where he followed other officers into a sub-committee meeting run by LTC Bennet Clark of the 35th Infantry Division.

On the afternoon of March 15, 1919 in Paris, France, Major E.F. Wood, U.S. Army and Temporary Secretary of the Temporary Committee opened the first official meeting of the *American Legion Caucus*. He explained to the assembled men, almost all officers:

> Early this year it was decided by G.H.Q. that it would be advantageous to get in personal touch with the point of view of the citizen soldiers of the A. E. F.:—with the drafted men of the National Army Divisions and with the volunteers of the Militia Divisions, as well as with their respective reserve and national guard officers.
>
> In order to bring this about, G. H. Q. decided to hold each month until further notice a meeting of some 20 or 30 National Guard and Reserve officers of field rank in order to obtain from them an expression as to the wants, inclination, and needs of the non-professional soldiers who constitute the vast majority of the present American Army."[2]

---

[2] American Legion, *Minutes, First meeting of the Caucus...* (Legion, 1920)

He went on to describe the committees and the business that lay before them.

The Paris Caucus. Photo courtesy Legion.org

Williams would later become a distinguished member of Harvey W. Seeds and share his stories as a witness to Legion history.

What Williams, LTC Clark and MAJ Wood couldn't know that afternoon was that this patriotic Veteran's organization would grow exponentially, filling a void for the more than 1.1 million Veterans who travelled overseas for service.

In Miami, Florida, on April 10, 1919, Mayor William P Smith, himself a Veteran, issued a call to all Veterans of World War I to form the *Dade County Association of Veterans of the World War.* The first meeting was at Miami's Chamber of Commerce offices, a fitting backdrop considering the relationship that the nascent organization and the city would have in the following years. 35 veterans attended and set in motion the work that would give rise to the Miami chapter of the largest Veteran's organization the world has ever seen.

By April 30 no dues had been collected and no finances had come to fruition, so a few of the officers that had been elected at the April 10 meeting signed a note from a local bank to finance the trip that would send Junius, (J.T.) Wigginton, former Commander of Company M, 124th Infantry, Florida National Guard and the adjutant, to the American Legion's national caucus. Major Robert

W. Ralston, a real estate salesman and investor, was nominated as first commander of the organization.

The committee adopted a preamble hauntingly similar to that of the national organization; "It shall be the purpose of the Dade County Association of Veterans of the World War to perpetuate the memory of those who gave their lives in the war, to carry their ideals for which they made the supreme sacrifice and to work for the moral, physical and financial betterment of its members."[3]

Newspapers around the country carried notices of the American Legion's upcoming organizational meeting, its formal founding. If you picked up a newspaper, you read about the *Veteran's organization*.

The American Legion's St Louis Caucus was held on 8-10 May 1919, after Dade County's *Association of Veterans* was already organized. During those meetings, the work that had been initiated in Paris was formalized. National officers were elected. Future convention sites were chosen and the now-famous preamble was adopted: "For God and Country we associate ourselves together for the following purposes..."

Only four other men from Florida (S.L. Lowry, Morris Givens, Harold McGuken, David Forster) went to the national convention and with Comrade Wigginton, they formed the Florida Department.[4]

On May 15, 1919, the Dade County Veterans met again and

---

[3] J.B. Williams, *History, Harvey W. Seeds Post No. 29,* (Miami, 1921)

[4] Florida District 6, *Florida District 6 History,* (http://fald6.org/district_history.php)

unanimously voted to affiliate themselves completely with the American Legion.

Charter Members of the *Dade County Veterans* and their service units (Members who were at the first meeting) are: Robert W. Ralston, 29th INF, William P. Smith, General Staff, Junius T. Wigginton, 64th INF, Henry G. Ralston, 37th INF, Guilford Green, 124th INF, Tom Gammage, 128th Field Artillery, J.C. Gramling, JAG, Arthur Keene, 156th INF, P.R. Scott, 17th Field Artillery, Raymond Forrest, 1st Army HQ, Frank Ashworth, Engineers, W.S. Gramling, Medical Corps, Adrian McCune, 124th INF, William Schneiderman, INF, J.E. Lind, QM, Joe Dillon, QM, H.G. Tuckerman, Navy, J.T. Harper, Navy, D.T. Davis, Navy, J.D. McVicar 30th INF, Harry Acker, 330th INF, D.L. O'Berry, 329th INF, James Gibbs, 156th Depot Brigade, J.S. Mulvihill, 6th Replacement DIV, G.L. Godley, 122nd INF, John B Williams, 330th INF, John R Long, 20th ENG, Jack Swattz, 150th INF, Ed Riley, 26th Hospital Corps, S. Hammer, Medical Corps, J.K. Fink, Roland Dean, Stuart Hall, M.H. George, S.A.T.C.

Charter Members of the post (Members who signed the application for charter of the American Legion in Florida, August 6, 1919) are: Harry C. Acker, H.E. Bratley, John C. Gramling, Joseph L Godley, Arthur G. Keene, L. E. Kloeber, L.C. Mount, D.N. Richardson, Dann C. Squires, R.L. Stephens, Frederick Sutner, J.B. Thomas, H.G. Tuckerman, Robert N. Ward, Junius T. Wigginton.

HARVEY SEEDS

Over the years, some people have wondered why Harvey Seeds has such a high post number, when it was clearly one of the first Legion posts organized in Florida. When the first state convention was held on June 6, 1919, it was rumored, that the boys from Miami were in the back of the room, cavorting and partying like they were known to do, and so when post numbers were assigned, they drew 29 just because they hadn't been paying attention.

Another rumor published in the *Legionnaire* magazine is that posts were asked to mail in applications and that post numbers were assigned as the mail was delivered and applications were literally picked out of a hat.

A more plausible explanation as to why Miami drew 29 is that the group had previously agreed, upon Comrade Wigginton's suggestion, that their namesake would be the first Soldier killed in action from Dade County and it took the War Department several months to validate that Harvey W. Seeds was indeed Miami's first doughboy killed in action in World War I.

Harvey Weber Seeds was born in Trenton, New Jersey to John Berkey Seeds and Elizabeth Weber Seeds in 1898. J.B. was a doctor and moved the family to Miami around 1916. Harvey was drafted into the U.S. Army shortly thereafter. Seeds was first assigned to Alpha Company, 324th Infantry, which was part of the 81st Division. [5] He was transferred to Delta Company, 9th Infantry

---

[5] *United States Army in the World War 1917-1919, (CMH, 1998)*
    http://www.history.army.mil/html/books/023/23-6/CMH_Pub_23-6.pdf. Accessed 29 OCT 2018.

Regiment, 2nd Division, the 'Indianhead Division,' which was committed to combat as part of AEF Forces in the spring of 1918.

Harvey Seeds arrived in Europe on June 20. He would be killed within a month.

The obituary read: "On the morning of July 18, 1918, on a sunny hillside in Chateau-Thierry, France, a well-thrown German grenade exploded over a machine gun emplacement, shattering it and taking the life of a handsome young man."

John and Elizabeth had no other children. John continued to practice medicine as he was one of only about 50 doctors in South Florida at the time and an important community asset.

She passed away in 1960. He passed in 1962.

HARVEY W. SEEDS

Private Harvey Weber Seeds. Photo courtesy Harvey W. Seeds archives.

CENTENNIAL HISTORY

IN MEMORY OF
★★★★★

HARVEY W. SEEDS

RANK
PRIVATE, U.S. ARMY

UNIT
9TH INFANTRY REGIMENT, 2ND DIVISION

DATE OF DEATH
JULY 18, 1918

COMMEMORATED IN PERPETUITY AT
AISNE-MARNE AMERICAN CEMETERY
BELLEAU, FRANCE

"Time will not dim the glory of their deeds."
— GENERAL JOHN J. PERSHING

Commemorative WWI casualty certificates can be found courtesy of the American Battle Monuments Commission website at https://www.abmc.gov

Harvey W. Seeds is memorialized at the Aisne-Marne American Cemetery in France and with a headstone at Woodlawn Cemetery, Miami.

During the Memorial Day service 1923, Commander Mills, in his Navy uniform, places a wreath at the newly installed headstone of Harvey W. Seeds.

FOUNDING FATHERS

At the 11th hour of the 11th day of the 11th month, bells tolled around the world signaling the signing of the armistice to end, *The Great War.*

America had mobilized over 4.3 million men. Over 234,000 were injured. Over 116,000 were killed or went missing in action. Those who survived, as many people who share the tragedies of war, were forever bound by their experiences.

It is important to note that 4674 Floridians made the ultimate sacrifice. Those were killed in action. An untold number died in training accidents or of diseases or other non-combat causes.

Although some Veterans immediately thrived upon return to civilian life, joining local government and civic organizations or starting businesses. Others suffered homelessness and worse.

The years after the *Great War* were full of new challenges and experiences for the men of that era. Many came home wounded or disabled. Old Victorian mores and values were prevalent in the South. Some men hid their wounds under clothing or had prosthetic limbs that were not functional but kept their injuries out of view. Civic society had a strange dilemma: More and more injured Soldiers were surviving their injuries as medical technology improved. Society wasn't sure how to integrate them.

Other men, undiagnosed, suffered silently from PTSD or what was referred to as shell-shock in its worst form. They, along with the community, benefited from the comradery and support that the Legion offered. They also benefited from the Service Officers in the Legion, who helped them with their Veteran's disability claims.

Congress passed the War Risk Insurance Act in 1917, creating the Bureau of War Risk Insurance, 'to pay compensation to disabled Veterans and the dependents of those who died..." The result was chaos. In tens of thousands of cases, the bureau failed to pay allotments and allowances rightfully due Veterans. There was no redress. [6] This benefit was constantly in the crosshairs of Legion national officers who constantly petitioned Congress for improvements and expansion.

> The spirit of the doughboy, his courage, character, values and ideals was the spirit tempered in the crucible of combat which formed the values of The American Legion as expressed so eloquently by the founders in the preamble to our constitution. We Legionnaires stand on the shoulders of giants who were the founders, all of whom were World War I veterans.[7]

The first 24 posts chartered in Florida at the June 6, 1919 Department meeting were, in numerical order: Titusville, Wauchula, Bartow, Lakeland, Tampa, Deland, Clearwater, Winter Haven, Jacksonville, Kissimmee, Arcadia, West Palm Beach, Tallahassee, St. Petersburg, Dade City, Gainesville, New Smyrna, Palmetto, Orlando, Marianna, Bradenton, Sarasota, Winter Park and Live Oak.

60 men were members of Harvey Seeds American Legion Post 29 in its first year. They came from all walks of life. Uniting, as Major Robert Ralston said to the Miami Herald, "...that they get a whack

---

[6] Marquis James, *A History of the American Legion*, (NY: William Green, 1923)

[7] John D. Monahan, *Proceedings of the 98th National Convention* (Nevada: American Legion, 2017)

at what they would have got had they stayed at home and not gone to war."

It was readily apparent early on that the first class of post members was replete with Miami's finest. E.K. Jaudon and Henry Ralston sat on the Miami Board of Health along with Dr. James Jackson when they pushed for the construction of what later became Miami's Jackson Memorial Hospital. Jaudon was a founding member of Post 29 and was Miami's county physician and superintendent of the charity hospital that pre-dated JMH. Ralston's brother, Robert Ralston, was a founding member and the post's first commander. He was also the developer of Miami's first skyscraper.

Other members were real estate developers, attorneys, businessmen and doctors, but regardless of finances or social status they affiliated themselves with the Legion and each other for the common good.

In an *Armistice Day*, later Veteran's Day, parade in 1919, *International Workers of the World,* (IWW) members, sometimes known as *Wobblies,* attacked a parade where Legionnaires were marching. *Wobblies* were known to have leftist leanings. They were vilified as Communists. The conflict set ablaze the *Red Scare* of 1919-1920 and pitted left vs. right.

In late 1919 Miami faced a union labor riot of its own. Mayor Smith notified the post members and they unanimously voted, "to respond individually or collectively, at any time the mayor summons for assistance of any kind to maintain law and order."[8] Luckily the strike did not materialize but the precedent was set.

---

[8] Arthur Keene, *Introduction-History Harvey W Seeds* in *History of Harvey W. Seeds Post No. 29,* (Miami: Review Print, 1960)

Dade County could call on a back-up civilian pool of trained men to quell civic disturbances

In a national meeting in November 1919, the American Legion formalized its unwavering support for the Boy Scouts and galvanized a relationship that stands to this day.

The Miami boys were making waves across the Legion early on. Comrade J.L. Billingsley of Harvey Seeds was elected Florida Department Commander in 1920.

On Memorial Day 1920, the post honored Veteran Bryan Padgett, who was re-buried with full honors. One of Miami's first VFW posts was later named for him.

With success, however, came competition; Homestead's John G. Salley post was chartered in 1919. In 1920, Comrade, Dr. Emerson Ayars helped charter Coconut Grove's Lindley De Garmo post. De Garmo was a member of the Army Air Service killed in WWI. Coral Gables post #98 was organized in 1925. In 1937 an all-female Legion post was chartered in Miami. It was named Poinsettia Post #113.

While Legionnaires are only members of one post at a time, Veterans had a myriad of social and service organizations to occupy their time: The Veterans of Foreign Wars chartered the William McAllister post in 1928. The Military Order of the World War, an officer's organization, was chartered by Comrade Charles Mills in Miami in 1934. As if that wasn't enough, Army and Navy Unions were chartered in the 30's, and a Dade County Council of the Legion as well as a Patriotic Observance Committee to help coordinate services of some of the other groups sprouted into existence.

Many Legionnaires were *40 & 8* members, Masons, Knights of Columbus (KC), Elks, Mahi's or Shriners, and Rotarians at the same time.

Throughout its early history the post enjoyed national attention. Former Secretary of State, William Jennings Bryan visited the post to speak on multiple occasions. He wintered in South Florida. President-elect Warren G Harding spent several weeks in Miami during the winter of 1921. He visited the post and spoke at a regular meeting.

In 1921 a group of American Legion members went back to France to visit newly erected war monuments. This was the prelude to the American Legion pilgrimages to come.

While segregated in its early years, the Legion admitted female Veterans. In 1921, the first two female post members were Lydia Marie Christiansen and Alice Flory Coursen.

Post Commander became a revered title. Leadership in the Legion was a great equalizer. One didn't have to be an officer, there were no boards, just a nomination from your peers and a simple election. In what was perhaps a propaganda device in search of the nomination for Post Commander in 1923, Charles Mills published and distributed copies of, *The American's Creed*, pictured herein. It worked. He was elected soon thereafter.

The American's Creed
By William Tyler Page

I believe in the United States of America as a government of the people, by the people, for the people; whose just powers are derived from the consent of the governed; a democracy in a Republic; a sovereign Nation of many sovereign States; a perfect Union, one and inseparable; established upon those principles of freedom, equality, justice and humanity for which American patriots sacrificed their lives and fortunes.

I therefore believe it is my duty to my Country to love it; to support its constitution; to obey its laws; to respect its flag; and to defend it against all enemies.

✯ ✯ ✯ ✯ ✯

As the Legion grew, however, they remained segregated, allowing each Department to make its own admission rules. Black Veterans protested ongoing segregation in New York in 1921, carrying signs and banners reading, "The Negro as a soldier has no peer," "The Negro won the war," "The Negro's fighting strength is not known."[9]

Legionnaires were not always on the right side of history, but they were on the side of good order and discipline. In 1921, KKK members abducted a popular black leader, Reverend Ritchie Higgs, in Miami's Coconut Grove neighborhood. Grove Police

---

[9] *Convention Parade of the U.N.I.A.*, Negro World, (1 August 1921), GP: III, 566

requested assistance from neighboring departments and the City of Miami armed the veterans of Harvey Seeds with rifles and machine guns to help keep order. Due to the Legion's assistance, major bloodshed was averted.[10]

In its early years, the post negotiated the purchase of over 200 burial plots at Miami's Woodlawn Cemetery, where they had previously raised a flagpole to honor Veterans. The Woodlawn plot became the final resting place for Past Commanders, Veterans who had wanted to be buried with Comrades or Veterans who had nowhere else to be buried.

Comrades O.A. Sandquist and W.A. Snow built the Woodlawn monument (initially, a short obelisk) at no charge to the post. Snow was post Adjutant in 1923.

---

[10] Claudrena N. Harold, *The Rise and Fall of the Garvey Movement in the Urban South, 1918–1942*, (New York, Routledge, 2007)

Woodlawn obelisk in its early form. Photo courtesy Harvey W. Seeds archive.

Past Commander (P/C) Mills dedicated the Harvey Seeds headstone at Woodlawn Memorial Park. He said, "I dedicate this monument to Harvey W. Seeds and with it I dedicate this post which bears his name to the eternal service of our country and the preservation of the memory of those who died, that liberty might not perish."

Through its first few years in existence, the post assisted over 300 veterans in filing benefits *relief cases*, what would soon be known as Veteran's claims.

In 1924 the Miami City Commission recognized the post's importance in the community and voted to deed a small parcel of land on Biscayne Boulevard to the post.[11]   The first post meetings had been held at the Chamber of Commerce offices, the Central School, War Camp Community Service office, the YMCA and even local restaurants when another meeting place wasn't available.

Always a Navy man, Commander at the time, Charles Mills suggested that a retired concrete ship be anchored in Biscayne Bay as the post headquarters. Miami Beach developer Carl Fisher donated the towing fee for the ship from New England. The plan floundered, however, when the ship arrived and Legionnaires realized that it was unsuitable for most of their activities.

By July 4, 1925, using member architects, member developers and member muscle, ground was broken ceremoniously on a two story structure (the first permanent post home) that included a rooftop party deck and which became the envy of many posts around the country. By the beginning of 1926, the post had over 1500 members.

---

[11] L.T. Kendrick, "Harvey W Seeds Post is Oldest in Florida", *Miami Herald* (September 28,1930), 32

The first post home was on the corner of Biscayne and NE 8 St, approximately across from where the American Airlines Arena stands today. Photo courtesy post archives.

The property had an empty lot behind it where boxing matches and minstrel shows were held. The fights brought needed funds for post activities. The minstrel shows, however, were a financial disaster. Boxing brought unwanted attention. Al Capone was arrested once, immediately after attending a Legion boxing match.

Having a building was a boon to the Legion and the community. The Miami chapter of the *United Spanish War Veterans* began meeting at the American Legion building in 1925, as did other organizations.

Later that year, post comrade Harvey R. Payne was elected Florida Department Commander. Past Commander Norris McElya was elected to represent Dade County in the Florida House of Representatives. The post's first commander, Robert Ralston, won election to Miami Beach City Council.

The American Legion petitioned Congress to fund round-the-clock guards for the Tomb of The Unknown Soldiers at Arlington in 1926.

THE BIG BLOW

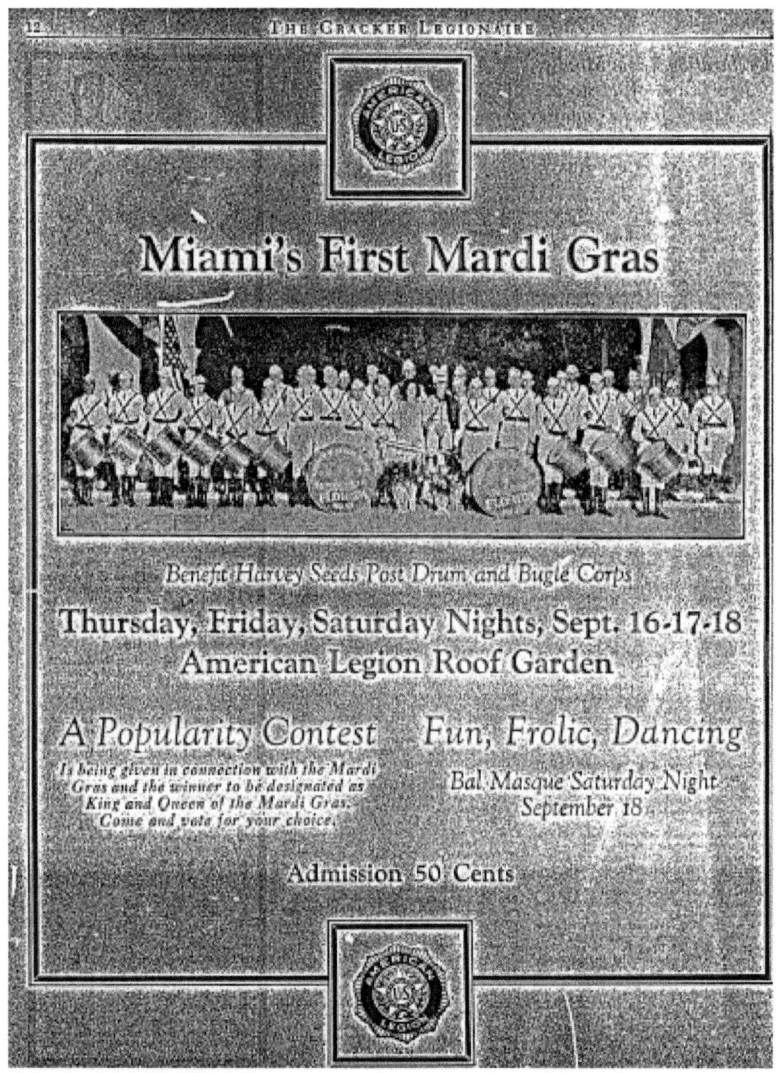

50 cents would have gotten you a rooftop view of the Great Miami Hurricane of 1926. Photo courtesy of Bob Zinko.

On the night of September 17, 1926, the post members were hosting a Mardi-Gras themed, three-day carnival at their downtown Miami headquarters located at 8th Street and Biscayne Blvd. It was a fundraiser to finance the drum corps trip to the national convention. Everyone liked to go on the rooftop of the building, where you could look south and see the growing Miami skyline on your right and Biscayne Bay on your left. It was supposed to be a three night event, but on Friday night it began raining steadily and as the party wound down, the winds picked up. "By midnight it was a full gale."[12]

If anyone had been able to stay on the roof of the post headquarters that night they would have seen the hurricane warning flag go up at about 11pm on the federal building, just a few blocks away. They would have seen an eight-foot storm surge pushing ships across Biscayne Boulevard and washing cars out to the bay. Looking west they would have seen some of the smaller buildings in the city begin to sway in the strong winds and they would not have seen Miami Beach as they looked east because it had been completely flooded over, as had the bridges that connected the barrier islands. Measurements would later reveal that the tide had exceeded 10.5 feet on the ocean side of Miami Beach.

The hurricane's eye passed over Miami and sightseers went out to survey the damage when the winds lulled, not realizing that they only had a few minutes to live. At about 6 am the winds stopped completely. By 6:47 the winds had shifted to the southeast and by 7:30 they were blowing as strong as 128 miles per hour.[13] Cars full of people were washed away when the back

---

[12] Richard Gray, *National Weather Service Weather Forecast Office Report (Miami, 1926)*, https://www.weather.gov/mfl/miami_hurricane

[13] Richard Gray, *National Weather Service Weather Forecast Office Report (Miami, 1926)*, https://www.weather.gov/mfl/miami_hurricane

side of the eye wall came ashore. 372 people were reported killed and over 6000 injured according to official accounts. Further north, hundreds drowned after the storm's deluge overcame an earthen dike near Lake Okeechobee.

The storm was later found to be a *Category 4* with winds gusting to 150 mph in some places. Most wood structures from Homestead to Boca Raton were razed, over 4700 homes were destroyed. Almost all telegraph and electrical wires and posts were down. Even sturdy concrete buildings are said to have swayed in the winds. One estimate put the price of property loss as high as $76,000,000.

Four days before the storm, the Cracker Legionnaire published a story describing the Florida Department as one large, 12,000 man post. It couldn't have been more prescient. Within thirty minutes of the storm's passing, Legionnaires began showing up for service.

"As soon as the winds subsided, in the afternoon, a number of members of the post reported to headquarters in the post home…..committees were appointed and everybody went to work," recalled Past Commander A.J. Cleary.[14]

Miami after the storm of 1926. Photo courtesy Library of Congress.

The Harvey Seeds Post did what military men and women do in times of crisis: They organized a response, which by some

---

[14] Feibelman, *History of Harvey W. Seeds..* , 11

accounts was more formidable than the local authorities could muster alone.

Mrs. Edwin Barker, wife of a post member said, "The Legion home presented a somber appearance with doctors and nurses administering to the injured where only a day before joyous revelers held sway."[15]   A photo in the *American Legion Monthly* magazine shows over a dozen cots in a room and the caption reads, "A corner of the clubhouse of Harvey W. Seeds Post, converted overnight from a dance hall to a hospital…"

There were reports of looting, as is common after hurricanes. Miami Police Lieutenant William J. McCarthy, a Legionnaire, enlisted 63 post members to serve as auxiliary police. James G Vaughn, another post member, provided horses from his, *Miami Riding Academy,* to the auxiliary policemen.

Rail lines were severed north of Palm Beach, so no relief would make its way to South Florida for a number of days. The National Guard, with many Legionnaires as members, mustered and began policing the streets.

City officials formed a *Citizens Relief Committee*, with 25 sub-committees. Past Commander, S.P. Robineau was chairman. Legionnaires were chairmen of 22 of the sub-committees.

Cliff Reeder, already a Past Commander and later Mayor of Miami, organized a soup kitchen which fed about 1500 relief workers daily. The post turned into a make-shift hospital where over 3000 patients were seen. 5000 people were given clothing. Once help arrived, the post continued relief work, making it a hub

---

[15] Feibelman, *History of Harvey W. Seeds..*, 10

for food and clothing distribution and health care. Over 7000 typhoid inoculations were distributed at the post in the weeks after the storm.

On September 29, the Miami Herald reported that Legionnaire, Dr John Lonroth, who had moved to Miami only three days before the storm, had organized the supply depot at the McAlister Hotel. Lonroth was a double amputee and worked non-stop for three days straight after the storm, ending up in the Legion field hospital himself for exhaustion. It's estimated that he had seen over 500 patients at the field hospital. "His wheelchair was his chariot."[16]

The post was so well organized and suited for the purpose that the Red Cross simply moved into the Legion post and ran their relief operations from there for the following six months.

The *Citizens Relief Committee* survived the storm relief efforts and was left intact as an arrangement between the county, the Legion, the Veterans of Foreign Wars (VFW), the Florida National Guard and Naval Reserve with support from the Miami Outboard Association and other commercial partners. Each group had specific responsibilities. Law enforcement would be supported by the Florida National Guard and members of the Harvey Seeds drum corps. Marine rescue would be handled by the Naval Reserve and supported by the VFW. Medical overflow could be handled at Harvey Seeds post home as it would be an emergency field hospital. The *Committee* had a truck, a doctor, nurse and emergency medical equipment at its disposal, along with agreements for ambulances and drivers.

---

[16] Herald Staff, "American Legion Busy, " Miami Herald (Sep 29, 1926), 4

R.V. Waters was elected Commander of Harvey Seeds later that year. City residents, now confident of the Legion's service abilities, voted him as President of the Biscayne Boulevard Association soon thereafter.

The *Great Miami Hurricane* left Miami a mess. "It squished the boom and started our depression three years early," said Miami historian Arva Parks.

The real estate boom was over. Many people left Florida and moved north looking for work and new homes. Some accounts said that as southbound relief trains dropped off supplies to rebuild the area, the trains were packed with passengers when they returned north, refugees of the storm.

SECOND AEF

The Harvey Seeds post in the 1920's, as it is today, was composed of men of differing interests and abilities. In 1923 the group was able to establish from within its membership, a drum corps, which became increasingly successful, not only as musical group, but as ambassadors for Miami. The Memorial Day parade of May 30, 1923 was their first reported public performance.

Harvey Seeds, American Legion Post #29 drum corps after winning the 1927 Legion drum corps championship, at the Eiffel Tower, Paris, France 1927. Photo courtesy post archives

The drum corps requested and received funding from the city of Miami as ambassadors of the burgeoning area. Local business giant, E.G. Sewell oversaw the Chamber of Commerce's advertising budget of over $170,000, a huge sum for that time and he saw fit to invest some of that money in the Veterans of Harvey W Seeds. In that year they participated in the American Legion National Convention in San Francisco.[17]

In 1926 they recruited Cesar La Monaca to become musical director of the group. La Monaca was a child prodigy and had toured America as a French Horn player, conductor and leader of a number of bands that embodied the John Phillip Sousa style of martial music, popular at the time.

---

[17] Herald Staff, "More than 1000 take part in Miami parade; Honor Seeds memory," Miami Herald, (November 13, 1923), 1

La Monaca had been a military musician during the *First World War* and had run several drum corps in Hollywood, Florida.

The November 10, 1926 Miami Herald ran several stories about life getting back to normal after the great storm: The University of Miami planned a friendly football game with the visiting University of Havana over Thanksgiving weekend. The Legion received their shipment of new overseas caps, orange colored with the Legion emblem on the front and orange blossoms on the side. They were getting ready for Paris.

For a few years the American Legion had been planning a mass return to Europe. In 1927 it came to fruition and the American Legion held its ninth annual convention in Paris in what was lauded as, "The second AEF invasion."[18] Legionnaires met in New York and embarked on passenger ships, which they virtually took over. The ship carrying the Florida clan, the S.S. Pennland, even published its own daily newspaper, filled with athletic event schedules, and bridge tournament results.

Unwilling to let an ocean get the best of them, Legionnaires held daily races at the *American Legion Turf Club* on the deck of the ship. Entertainment was plentiful.

The *flagship* of the flotilla, S.S. Leviathan, carried General John J. 'Blackjack' Pershing as well as Past Commander Charles Mills, who was then *Chef de Chemin de Fer* of the national *40 & 8*.

Photos of the drum corps marching down the Champs Elysees and past the Arc de Triumph adorned the post's halls for decades to follow.

---

[18]Legion Staff, American Legion Magazine (American Legion), https://archive.legion.org/

Harvey W Seeds drum corps leads the Florida delegation through the Arc de Triomphe, Paris, France 1927. Photo courtesy Harvey W Seeds archives.

Once in France, the Legion doubled down on its commitment to, "Never Forget." While there was a huge celebratory parade in Paris, which made international news, ceremonies at Verdun and other cemeteries were notably more somber. The French lit torches of friendship and shared meals and war stories with the Americans. The groups toured the still-existing trenches at several battlefields. Many battlefields had been left almost completely untouched during the interim years.

When the formalities were complete, the drum corps competition saw Harvey W. Seeds, Post #29 win the first ever American Legion drum corps championship on foreign soil and the first of Harvey Seeds' dynastic drum corps run.

They were invited back to the barracks of the French Republican Guard where they were toasted with champagne and cake.

Drum corps color guard stands at attention as a wreath is presented in front of a monument, Paris, France, 1927. Photo courtesy post archives.

Miami and Florida gained more worldwide publicity through the victory of the drum and bugle corps in Paris than through any other channel." [19]

The selfless acts of the class of 1926 drum corps brought great credit upon the organization as well as national and international attention that would help them in the upcoming years.

---

[19] Herald Staff, "Miami gains much by Legion's drum corps ", Miami Herald, (October, 16, 1927), 32

Legionnaires tour WWI fortifications, France, 1927.Photo courtesy post archives.

Writer Rufus Steele later told the Miami Legionnaire magazine, "It was more – far more- than the mere winning of a coveted honor. – it was the triumphing of young Americans who are good Soldiers in peace as well as in war"

THE DEPRESSION

With all communications to the north blocked beyond Fort Lauderdale, a relief expedition composed of fifteen members of Harvey Seeds American Legion post left by automobile for the area over which the storm is believed to have swept.[20]

In 1928, just before the Department convention was to take place in Ft Pierce, another hurricane swept across West Palm Beach with 145 mph winds. Over 1700 homes were destroyed in Palm Beach alone and the storm caused a breach of Lake Okeechobee, which flooded hundreds of square miles, drowning over 2500 people.

P/C A.J. Cleary took the first team as far as they could get into West Palm Beach. They cleared roads and railways on the way and dropped off supplies then returned to Miami within 24 hours to organize a relief train that set out the following day.

Inside the stricken area, citizens had used the nearest Legion post as a shelter, saving dozens of lives.

Legionnaires went to work immediately, sending supplies and men to work even before the Red Cross arrived. Legionnaires helped collect bodies and bury the dead.

Legion auxiliaries held a special meeting to organize their relief efforts. Before that meeting they had already put out requests for clothing and monetary donations to be collected at Miami's Central School. By September 23, the Herald reported that the Harvey Seeds Auxiliary along with those from Hialeah and the

---

[20] Associated Press, "Relief Expedition," *Oshkosh Daily Northwestern*, (September 17, 1928), 21

Coconut Grove posts had travelled to the Deerfield Beach post to set up a forward relief station, to be occupied until the Red Cross could take over.

The 1928 storm was catastrophic to farmers and poor laborers in rural Palm Beach and central Florida. Seeing the ravages of that storm, many posts petitioned the Florida Governor to create an emergency fund for relief in the face of future Florida disasters.

Later that year, the auxiliary raised $2000 and shipped over 28,500 pounds of donated clothing to the destitute and homeless after flooding in Memphis and Little Rock.

Past Commander C.H. Reeder was elected Mayor of Miami in the election of 1928 and took office in 1929.

The drum corps went on to win another national championship in San Antonio. They celebrated success by visiting President Herbert Hoover at the White House. It was the second time they had photos with him. While he was President-elect, he had come through Miami on his way to Cuba.

October 29, 1929 was *Black Tuesday*, a financially devastating day for the stock market and the beginning of terrible unemployment, which reached 25% nation-wide.

From 1929 to 1930, as *The Great Depression* gripped America, the post improved and expanded the memorial at Woodlawn Cemetery. Beyond the bronze plaques, four statues were erected around the obelisk, representing different branches of military service. Post members were the models for sculptor, Robert Paul Goldie, who donated his services and adorned the obelisk.

Kathleen K. Perigo, City of Miami nurse and Army Nurse Corps

Veteran was the model for the nurse. Harvey E. Howard was the doughboy. He was an anti-aircraft officer and drum major and captain of the drum corps. P/C and Past Adjutant, Joe Frank was the Marine and William Howard Christian, who was later the first post member killed in WWII, was the model for the sailor.

Unemployed did not equal idle to the American Legion.

The Legion became a valuable resource within the community during these hard times. The drum corps would practice almost every day, giving young men something to do while they couldn't find work. City leaders again decided to use the corps as ambassadors to continue to inspire people from around the country to come to Florida and invest in the state.

Comrade Joe Frank was elected Commander of the Dade County Council of Veterans, an organization dedicated to coordinating Veteran's benefits for Miami-Dade residents. The council took up issues with legislature on behalf of at least eight Legion posts and thousands of Veterans.

Robert Paul Goldie sculpted the four figures on the Legion memorial. Photo courtesy post archive.

In the 1930's, the post was able to petition the government through the WPA's Federal Music Project to create jobs for unemployed musicians as drum corps instructors. A full staff headed by Captain Thomas J. Kelly, Commander, 265th Coast Artillery, Florida National Guard was formed. He taught marching. Music was headed by Cesar La Monaca, Warrant Officer and Musical Director of the 265th Coast Artillery Band of the Florida National Guard. The group had a quartermaster and section heads. Veterans mingled with Guardsmen and even some professional musicians who were neither. Marching drum corps were an immensely popular pastime in the 30's and 40's.

Past Commander Virgil Ector was elected to the state boxing commission. A number of Legion posts had members on the commission. Legionnaires felt they were better able to manage legal fights if they participated in the legislation and supervision of all aspects of the sport, which was not only a pastime but a fundraiser for the Legion.

A 1931 retrospective article in the department newspaper describes a memo written to all departments by Frank Samuel, national Assistant Adjutant. "National headquarters sent out a notice that the inter-departmental membership derby… in competition for the Lindsley trophy… is on." Although Florida won the previous year for the greatest membership growth, the notice described a, "dark horse," that could take them over.

Goldie finishes the Sailor statue, modeled after W.H. Christian, a post member who was later killed in WWII. Photo courtesy Harvey Seeds archives.

Florida Legionnaires rose to the occasion and brought the trophy home that year, and for six years afterwards. The Florida Department subsequently presented Samuel with a photo of an orange colored horse and named their department newspaper *The Orange Horse*, after Florida's greatest export at the time, oranges.

The legacy of Legion journalism goes back to July 4, 1919 when the *American Legion Weekly* began publishing. In 1926 the weekly was substituted by the monthly which ran until 1937. The monthly turned into the *American Legion Magazine*. In 1935 a tabloid emerged devoted entirely to news and non-fictional Legion activities. It merged with *American Legion Magazine* in 1949, which publishes to this day.

On September 2, 1931, Volume 1, number 1 of the *Miami Legionnaire* was published as a bi-weekly. Roger Carter, the Post Commander at the time, was the editor. This publication, the first issue said, "is for the purpose of keeping the officers and members of Harvey W. Seeds Post in closer contact, and do its share towards the upbuilding of the post...The Legion moves forward, a great peace-time army in the service of God and country."

The *Cracker Legionnaire* was a semi-monthly publication and began about the same time. Through the years post publications have taken many forms, including a one page fold-over, a multi-page newspaper, with advertisers, a flyer and most recently, an electronic e-mail.

William P Davis narrowly defeated Thomas J Kelly for election as post commander for 1931-1932. His philanthropic efforts focused around the American Children's home and a Legion dental clinic.

If you are old enough, you will remember that public schools had in-house physicals many years ago. Comrade Davis was pivotal in making sure the physicals included dental exams.

By the end of 1932 the Harvey Seeds post was submitting Veteran's benefits claim for Veterans of *The World War*, the Spanish American War, the Philippine Insurrection and even for the few remaining Civil War Veterans. 2231 claims were processed that year.

During the late 20's and through the 30's, the post was the official auto tag agency for Dade County. Tag sales, boxing and bingo allowed the Legion to raise money for post services.

Past Commander Charles A Mills was elected National Vice Commander 1932-1933.

During *the Depression*, the national American Legion found more than 300,000 jobs for Veterans and also helped almost 200,000 others with temporary jobs.

In times of peace, the Legion kept trying to find its place in American society. National Commander at the time, Louis Johnson noted in 1933 that the Legion would be a good partner for law enforcement in the fight against organized crime. Mayor Anton Cermak of Chicago, coincidentally, had vowed to eradicate all organized crime in his city before the following year's World's Fair. Some people thought that this promise put a price on Cermak's head, as organized crime was rampant in Chicago at the time.

Cermak travelled to meet president-elect Franklin Roosevelt in Miami in 1933.

The Legion participated in almost every major event in South Florida. When Giuseppe Zangara shot Cermak and barely missed Roosevelt, the Legion was in the park. The drum corps had performed before Roosevelt arrived and Legionnaires assisted with crowd control for the event.

A group of Legionnaires tackled Zangara and held him down until the Secret Service and local police whisked him away. [21] Mayor Cermak had previously hosted the drum corps during their visit to Chicago in 1931. They had made him an honorary member.

After he passed on in Miami, they provided a funeral procession and were pallbearers for his casket.[22]

P/C Mills escorts President and Mrs. Hoover as they review Boy Scouts in Miami. Photo courtesy post archives.

---

[21]British Movietone,"Assasination attempt on FDR-1933…," www.youtube.com/watch?v=SUNrv1F09-g. Accessed July 8,2018

[22] British Pathe, "Cermak goes to final rest," www.youtube.com/watch?v=v2Lr-WDZcYA . Accessed July 8,2018

Screen shot from video showing Harvey Seeds drum corps at the head of Cermak's funeral procession on the way to the train. Photo courtesy British Pathe/Youtube.

The Florida Department of the American Legion held its 1933 convention in Havana, Cuba. The corps showed up in a chartered sea plane. Havana Post number 1 played host to the Florida gang, organizing a parade and a musical exchange with the Havana police band.

Harvey Seeds' Drum Corps won its second international competition, bringing home another state championship, but they were later disqualified at the national competition.

1933 was also the year of the first Orange Bowl game. Before corporate sponsorship and huge college budgets, the Orange Bowl committee counted on Harvey Seeds and the Greater Miami Boys Drum Corps to entertain in every parade.

The drum corps shows up in style in Havana, on a charter seaplane. Photo courtesy post archives.

"I remember my father one year marched the Orange Bowl parade about four times, "said Jean La Monaca McNamee, daughter of Cesar La Monaca.[23] He was the musical director for the Harvey Seeds drum corps as well as the *Miami Boys* drum corps and the 265th Coast Artillery Band, Florida National Guard.

At the same time, Past Commander Virgil Ector assumed charge of the Dade County Jail as Chief Deputy. It was just another chapter in the many that intertwined Harvey Seeds members and public service positions.

On Armistice Day 1933, Miami held a huge parade for Veterans. Nearby a separate Colored War Veterans parade drew African-American Veterans, church members, members of fraternal orders and the Miami Colored Chamber of Commerce. Harvey

---

[23] Interview with Jean McNamee, June 16, 2016

Seeds would occasionally provide ceremonial support for the funeral services of colored Veterans.

By the end of 1933, post member and state representative S.P. Robineau was advocating for the legalization of gambling in Florida. Robineau had his hands in many efforts. He was crucial in obtaining title to the parcel of land on Biscayne and NE 66 St, the *Tee House Plantation*, so named because the shape of the house was similar to the letter T. The house had a sordid history and belonged to a bar owner who passed away several years earlier. It was built for entertaining and it suit the Legion perfectly.

The T- House plantation was a sprawling 45 acre waterfront property just north of the previous home and of downtown Miami. There was space for the drum corps and baseball team to practice and lots of parking. There was a dock, a garage, multiple meeting rooms. It was perfect for the post at the time. Although there are rumors that it was purchased for $1, it cost the post about $18,500 to purchase the property, which the post didn't have, but they immediately sold a 4 acre parcel to put money in the bank and pay for taxes and improvements.

Still a phenomenal deal!

Easterly view of the T House. Photo courtesy Harvey Seeds archives.

The Legion post property from 1933 to 1966 was celebrated as one of the best in the country. Photo courtesy Harvey Seeds archives.

1934 brought the American Legion Convention to Miami. In order to vest politicians in the events, Governor Dave Sholtz was named honorary president and Mayor E.G. Sewell was named honorary chairman of the board of the convention corporation. The 1934 convention was so popular that there were several motions to make Miami the permanent convention home for the American Legion. None were successful. Above is an excerpt from the Miami Herald dated 21 October 1934 and found in our archives.

Mayor of Chicago, Edward J Kelly noted, " The greatest service the American Legion can perform for its country during the coming year is to throw its solid support behind President Franklin D Roosevelt and his program for reconstruction, " in an interview at

Miami Surrenders To the Legion

TWENTY years ago the world was plunged into war. It was European in inception. It would not involve the United States directly; America would keep out of that baptism of blood. So we were told. So we believed.

But the United States was snared in the red web. Billions of dollars. Millions of men. Over there the boys went. Singing, cheering. And over the top. Fighting. Dying. Then victory. Armistice. Peace. Spasms of joy. Madness of happiness. When the heroes came marching home.

And now Miami welcomes this army of heroes—The American Legion. The city and state salute them. In memory and honor of the past. In hopes for the future. A mighty organization, a nation, is here represented in convention assembled. History unfolds. With the tramp of feet, the beat of drums, the flutter of the flag. Hats off.

Veterans all. Veterans in experience, in strength, in knowledge. But still youthful, now in the prime of life. Once they fought bravely for the principles of democracy and won. They faced and solved that crisis in 1918.

Again there is a crisis to be confronted and battled. Again there is the same need for loyalty to the land of our fathers, to liberty, democracy, the constitution, the preservation of a free people, our common rights for a century and a half.

Legionnaires are patriots. Patriots in war. Patriots in peace. Unselfish patriotism is essential if any nation is to survive. That demands sacrifice and service. And faith.

Yes, the Stars and Stripes are still there waving on high. May Old Glory never be lowered. It is in your trust—The American Legion. The nation looks to you.

Miami greets you gladly. She is proud of what you have done, proud of the honor bestowed upon her by this visitation. She wishes you a merry time. That you may return again and again. Even dig in for a permanent stay. Miami surrenders. To the soldiers of war and of peace.

the Legion conference.[24]

Hoover had a shaky relationship with Veterans at the outset of his administration.

He sent Soldiers against the *Bonus Army* Veterans in 1932 when they protested for Veteran's benefits in Washington, but Roosevelt had vetoed the bonus that was eventually paid to Veterans by Congressional override.

The *Labor Day Hurricane* struck the Florida Keys in 1935, where many World War I Veterans were working on building a rail line to the island chain as one part of the reconstruction program that Roosevelt promoted. In his book, *Last Train to Paradise*, author Les Standiford describes the carnage of what was probably the most powerful storm to ever hit the U.S, with winds thought to have reached 200 miles per hour.

"Survivors... told chilling tales of men disemboweled by jagged sheets of roofing...skulls crushed by boulders flying through the air like pebbles...faces literally blasted down to bone by the driving sand."[25]

Almost half the population between Miami and Key West, over 400 people, are thought to have died in the storm.

Members of Harvey Seeds were moved by news of the casualties. They mobilized quickly and assisted in the recovery of the victims. P/C J.K. Williams took a team of Legionnaires to Lower Matecumbe Key, where they ferried dead and wounded with the

---

[24] Miami Herald, Harvey Seeds Post is 1st in Florida, (21 Oct 1934), 15

[25] Les Standiford. *Last Train to Paradise*.(NY,PenguinRandomHouse,2003), 238

help of men from the VFW. Over 259 Veterans were killed. 124 were transported to Miami hospitals with injuries. The tropical heat began to decay the dead almost immediately and a huge rush began to inter bodies. The Keys simply did not have enough burial spaces.

The Florida Emergency Relief Administrations, which the Legion had petitioned into existence, provided graves at Woodlawn Cemetery in Miami, adjacent to the Harvey Seeds plot. Later the post requested to manage the graves in perpetuity.

In the ensuing panic and lack of coordination, some of the dead were buried where they were found. Others were massed into funeral pyres and cremated. 170 Veterans were not accounted for. Some were cremated without proper funeral honors, some without being identified correctly. To the dismay of Veterans to this day, they are not accounted for properly in marked graves.

The post raised funds for the hurricane memorial that was later erected in memory of all those killed in the storm. Before 1937 was over, the post took the lead in obtaining $3,779 as a contribution (for the Keys Hurricane Memorial). The finished cost was around $12,000. The memorial was designed by the Florida Division of the Federal Art Project and was constructed by the Works Progress Administration (WPA).[26]

In a remarkable break from the usual expressions of resolute Americanism, Legion leaders were incensed that no one was held responsible for the inability to evacuate the Veterans from the Keys before the storm. In the end, the sentiment was that the

---

[26] Jerry Wilkinson,"Florida Keys Memorial," www.keyshistory.org/hurrmemorial.html, Accessed July 8, 2018

federal government did not care for this generation of Veterans, the *Bonus Army.*

An extremely quick federal investigation called the event, "an unfortunate act of God." The VA created a report for the President and the FERA conducted an investigation as well. They both ended up with differing tallies of dead, buried and their final dispositions. A confounding fact was that the storm was so massive that bodies were found months later and many miles away.

The Legion commissioned an independent investigation that found, "inefficiency, indifference and ignorance," in the WPA and work camp management. The adversarial rift between the Legion and the VA became painfully obvious.

Legion leaders continued to build its emergency relief fund with the help of the Auxiliary a full 50 years before FEMA existed, painfully aware that the U.S. government and the Red Cross were sometimes slow and improperly positioned to act in cases of civic emergency.

A flood of the Ohio River in 1937 left almost a million people homeless in Pennsylvania and Illinois. The Legion asked for posts to raise $20,000 in cash or goods. The Harvey Seeds Auxiliary raised over $85,000 in a few weeks and donated it to those stricken by disaster.

The American Legion's Nineteenth Annual Convention was held in New York, N.Y. on September 20-23, 1937. With palpable tensions growing in Europe, the Legion went back for the *American Legion 1937 Foreign Pilgrimage.* Some called it AEF III. This time, over 5500 Legionnaires and their families boarded ships heading to France, Italy and several other countries immediately after the convention in NY.

In the courtyard of *Les Invalides*, where Napoleon had once decorated his officers, the French awarded American Legionnaires for their sacrifices and support. General Pershing was honored with an equestrian statue unveiled at Versailles. He posed for a photo with corps mascot, Louise Otter after the ceremony.

The King of England granted an unprecedented audience to the American Legion National Commander, Daniel Doherty and his entourage.

The French Republican Guard welcomed Legionnaires to their barracks. The French hosted celebrations every night. Doherty later said the third AEF, "...served to bring a fuller appreciation of the tremendous price paid in service and sacrifice that democracy and liberty might be perpetuated….the futility of war and the blessings of peace."

No one could have known that just a couple of years later some of them would fight the Germans side-by-side.

After he had toured cemeteries, battlefields and monuments, Past National Commander Harry Colmery said, "Their task is done. Ours remains before us."

The world was in tumult.

THE DRUMS OF WAR

A 1937 Armistice Day speech by, "Colonel Williams," formerly of the Canadian Army warned a Miami crowd that there were over 2.6 million Communists in America. He assailed women's suffrage, the repeal of Prohibition and the Child Labor Movement. In sentiment that rings particularly true today, J.K. Williams, department Committee Member and Vice Commander of the post took the podium after Williams and warned the crowd that, "debunking history is no way to create nationalism today."[27]

There were a lot of deep-seeded opinions on both sides of the issue. Communism was a bad word. Fascists poised themselves as the answer to brutal Socialist revolutions around the world. America tried to remain neutral.

Comrade Wallace H Smith had a heart attack while driving and passed to his reward on July 24, 1938. Some accounts regarded him as the most wounded man in the AEF. He had 132 wounds, including a punctured lung (later removed) when he was rescued from the Chateu Thierry battlefield in 1918. Smith was a bugler and well-regarded member of the drum corps and continued to play his horn with only one lung.

A few post members attended Smith's funeral at Arlington National Cemetery. They saw the funeral honors afforded all Veterans at Arlington and brought the concept back to Miami to form the Dade County Guard of Honor.

The 1939-1940 World's Fair invited the Miami Boys Drum Corps to Flushing Meadows New York in what was one of the last major

---

[27] Miami Herald, *Armistice Speaker Assails Communism* (1937)

events the group would participate in before America entered World War II. The Miami Boys joined a 1500-mile long caravan from Miami to Boston which included Legionnaires travelling to the national convention. The group distributed two carloads full of coconuts, a carload of oranges and 5000 cigars in promotion of Florida industries on their way north.

Miami celebrated its 43rd birthday as a city later that same year. The drum corps, its numbers dwindling due to the draft, provided the celebratory music at Bayfront Park.

As Dr. Anthony Atwood explained in his doctoral thesis, "A State of War:...", between 1939 and 1940 the , "geostrategic concerns of place and space," seemed to thrust Florida into the middle of everyone's war plans.

The S.S. St Louis steamed off the coast with German Jewish refugees who were not allowed to disembark in Cuba and were not allowed to dock in the U.S. because of American neutrality at the time.

The German warship *Arauca* sought refuge from a British warship in Port Everglades, almost causing an international incident.

By 1940, post meeting minutes describe the Legion post building as being in disrepair and discussions began about renovations. Some of the more far-flung ideas included adding a bowling alley and pistol range on the property.

Those never came to fruition. Instead, they ended up patching and painting the band shell and re-paving the dance floor. They moved the bar and replaced gutters and downspouts.

At the same time, the post was able to put together a, "Trophy

Room," which held a pictorial account of and memorabilia belonging mostly to the drum corps, but ranging into other post activities, such as photos of all the Past Commanders and Auxiliary Presidents.

The trophy room was filled with symbols of the post's achievements. Photo courtesy post archives.

The post initiated participation in the Boys State program and sponsored four young men to go to Tallahassee. The post, along with other Dade County posts, petitioned Congress to fund ROTC as part of the curriculum in every high school in America.

Soon, daily operational concerns seemed irrelevant as Germany invaded country after country.

At the time Florida held only two percent of the country's population, however, as the draft began in September and the nation was mobilized, nearly one in eight Floridians went into uniform.[28]

September 1941 saw the last pre-war national convention in Milwaukee.

One of the curiosities of a Veteran's organization is its members' pride and willingness to share their stories with each other and the organization. Among the many items stored in three separate rooms at the old post building was a citation for George Rodearmel, Navy Quarterman Rigger. He was cited for, "most efficient action and unusual presence of mind," on December 7, 1941 during the Japanese attack on Pearl Harbor.

Members of the post have included a NASA photographer, newsroom editor, and several politicians. They left us many photographs of military units, citations (both military and civilian) and even an aircraft carrier yearbook.

Past Commander Kelly ran and lost the post of city tax collector. Past Commander Mills joined the Committee on Subversive Propaganda in 1941. He was charged with keeping Miami residents informed among rumors of horse meat being fed to military members in lieu of beef and German spies coming ashore all over Florida.

In 1941 Congress amended the National Defense Act of 1916 to authorize state defense forces following the federalization of most National Guard units. Florida's Legislature enacted statutes to organize Florida's Defense Force, with headquarters in St. Augustine and seven battalions organized statewide to include a

---

[28] Dr. Anthony Atwood, *A State of War: Florida from 1939 to 1945,* (Miami: FIU,2012)

total force of 1,990 officers and enlisted men. In 1943, the organization was re-designated the Florida State Guard.

A great many Florida State Guard were men too old or otherwise disqualified for active military duty. Many of them were Legionnaires. They found many ways to support the war effort. All of the men who were old enough, performed guard duty during the blackouts in downtown Miami or at the *Filter Center,* a military clearing house for aircraft observation calls.

Legionnaires, all volunteers, mustered as Florida State Guards in support of the defense of the homeland during WWII. Photo courtesy post archives.

World War I Veterans understood duty and they were ready when the nation needed them during World War II, even if they couldn't fight. They organized civil support teams. Where the drum corps used to perform for trophies, they now began raising funds for war bonds. The post began recycling. They gathered all usable metals, old paper and everything of value. It's believed that some of the post's pre-WWII documents were destroyed at this time.

State Guard volunteers drill with wood rifles.

Newspapers, radio, and travel were controlled; gasoline, tires, shoes and food were rationed.[29]

President Roosevelt came through South Florida a number of times before the war. He used the area as a jumping off point for trips to the Caribbean to watch naval exercises and once even anchored off the coast of Martinique, where a Vichy French contingent had enough ships and sailors to worry the President.

---

[29] Atwood, 2012

If the Vichy French had threatened the Panama Canal, Florida had the closest massing of naval forces that could defend it. It was understood that a single well placed Axis torpedo could cripple the canal and the movement of ships, troops and goods from Atlantic to Pacific and vice-versa.

America expected Germany to strike first but Japan launched the attack on, "day that will live in infamy, "December 7, 1941. America was surprised but not unprepared and Floridians were in the thick of things from the beginning.

Florida was pivotal in the movement of aerial assets through South America and across the Atlantic to Africa. Only the largest of planes could make the trans-Atlantic flight and there was no aerial refueling at the time. It took less time to fly a plane through the Caribbean and across to Africa than it did to ship it across the Atlantic and risk losing it to German submarines, but it was perilous.

Soon, over 85,000 trainers and trainees were working at military sites throughout Florida. Twenty naval air stations and forty seven Army airfields were completed or under construction in the state early on in the war.

Tallahassee International Airport, Jacksonville International Airport, Orlando International Airport, Tampa International Airport, Miami International Airport, and Fort Lauderdale International Airport were all military airfields later donated to the civilian community. Every airport in the State was either created in the war, or enhanced enormously by it.[30]

---

[30]Atwood, 2012

Chief William H. Christian was the first member of the post to die in active service on February 7, 1942. He is buried at the Legion plot at Woodlawn. He was the model for the sailor on the Legion monument that stands forever near his remains.

By March of that year, 103 former members of the Greater Miami Drum Corps were in the military. Past Commander Charles Mills became Vice Chairman of the Dade County Red Cross and allied many of his external efforts with the Legion's. Mills had been pivotal in assuring that the Navy had permanent assets in the South Florida area in the years leading up to the war and kept his connections with senior military leadership, to the benefit of Miami.

Comrade Samuel S. McCahill was elected Department Commander in 1942.

On June 27, 1942, LTC Sam Brabson, Executive Officer of the fighter command school on Miami Beach asked all tap rooms, bars and restaurants to stop serving alcohol after 11:30 pm each night. "We are up to our necks in this war now and all officers and enlisted men must remain in condition to perform their duties, "Brabson declared to newspapers. [31]

The idyllic tropical waters of Florida soon became training grounds for men who would eventually end up on less hospitable tropical islands in the Pacific, fighting Japan.

Throughout the war, Florida was used as a launching point for Project Aguila, Project X and other missions to support unlikely far away allies in Burma, India, Bataan and China.

American Legion posts during World War II held letter-writing

---

[31] Miami Herald, 1942

drives and hosted patriotic events. They focused on building community support for the country and the fight. As a body, the Legion advocated for the GI Bill and new Veteran's benefits programs. While fiercely patriotic, they also expressed differences of opinion with President Roosevelt. Sometimes, however, they were on the wrong side of history. In a misguided wave of nationalism, they advocated for the deportation of all Japanese from the US.[32]

Comrade Joe Frank was elected Florida Department Commander in 1944.

Mrs. Seeds, with a Gold Star Flag hanging in her living room, and a picture of Harvey Seeds on the mantle, reviews the Miami Herald, circa 1943. Photo courtesy archives.

---

[32] Legionnaire 1943

The S.S.Merrick, Liberty Ship display, containing photographs of the ship, the first flag flown over her as well as the cover for the champagne bottle used to christen her. Photo by author.

" The post and its Auxiliary unit set out in the Third War Loan drive to sell enough Bonds to finance a Liberty Ship and rolled up a total sales of $6,100,000—just about three times the goal fixed, In the Fourth War Loan campaign an additional $5,000,000 was added to the total. As a result, the name of George E. Merrick, honoring the developer of Coral Gables, was assigned a vessel by the U. S. Maritime Commission and the launching exercises were turned over to Harvey Seeds Post and its Auxiliary. "[33]

Legion members who were yet undrafted or ineligible to serve maintained the drum corps, color guard and raised funds during bond drives. Photo courtesy post archives.

Even though the U.S. Maritime Commission had curtailed ship launching ceremonies in light of the dozens of ships that were launched every day during the war, the Legion celebrated the S.S.

---

[33] Legionnaire 1944

Merrick with a christening and a plaque. Those items, along with a flag and the cover for the bottle used to christen the ship are on loan to the Coral Gables History Museum.

The Serviceman's Readjustment Act of 1944, also known as the G.I. Bill was signed into law by President Roosevelt on June 22, 1944. Arguably the Legion's greatest contribution to law and Veteran's rights, this act secured post-war civilian training, home financing and educational benefits for returning Veterans.

On February 19, 1945, Private First Class Douglas Jacobson came ashore at Iwo Jima with 3rd Battalion, 23rd Marines, 4th Marine Division. A week later he would forever leave his mark in history through his ferocious actions on the battlefield in one of the bloodiest campaigns in Marine history.

The citation reads:

> For conspicuous gallantry and intrepidity at the risk of his life above and beyond the call of duty while serving with the 3d Battalion, 23d Marines, 4th Marine Division, in combat against enemy Japanese forces during the seizure of Iwo Jima in the Volcano Island, 26 February 1945. Promptly destroying a stubborn 20mm. antiaircraft gun and its crew after assuming the duties of a bazooka man who had been killed, Pfc. Jacobson waged a relentless battle as his unit fought desperately toward the summit of Hill 382 in an effort to penetrate the heart of Japanese cross-island defense. Employing his weapon with ready accuracy when his platoon was halted by overwhelming enemy fire on 26 February, he first destroyed 2 hostile machinegun positions, then attacked a large blockhouse, completely neutralizing the fortification before dispatching the 5-man crew of a second pillbox and

exploding the installation with a terrific demolitions blast. Moving steadily forward, he wiped out an earth-covered rifle emplacement and, confronted by a cluster of similar emplacements which constituted the perimeter of enemy defenses in his assigned sector, fearlessly advanced, quickly reduced all 6 positions to a shambles, killed 10 of the enemy, and enabled our forces to occupy the strong point. Determined to widen the breach thus forced, he volunteered his services to an adjacent assault company, neutralized a pillbox holding up its advance, opened fire on a Japanese tank pouring a steady stream of bullets on 1 of our supporting tanks, and smashed the enemy tank's gun turret in a brief but furious action culminating in a single-handed assault against still another blockhouse and the subsequent neutralization of its firepower. By his dauntless skill and valor, Pfc. Jacobson destroyed a total of 16 enemy positions and annihilated approximately 75 Japanese, thereby contributing essentially to the success of his division's operations against this fanatically defended outpost of the Japanese Empire. His gallant conduct in the face of tremendous odds enhanced and sustained the highest traditions of the U.S. Naval Service.

Jacobson later told the New York Times, "'I don't know how I did it, I had one thing in mind -- getting off that hill." [34]

Jacobson later moved to Miami where he joined the Florida National Guard and was this post's first Medal of Honor recipient member.

On May 8, 1945, Germany surrendered.

---

[34] Richard Goldstein, *Douglas T. Jacobson, a Hero of Iwo Jima, Is Dead at 74*, (NY Times, Sep 18, 2000)

On September 2, 1945, a Japanese delegation formally signed surrender documents aboard the USS Missouri in Tokyo Bay.

The Governor of Florida issued a proclamation of victory. He declared a solemn commemoration for the 24-hour period to follow.

The proclamation urged all liquor package stores, bars, tap rooms, juke joints and other places dispensing alcoholic beverages to remain closed during that period. Across the State Floridians went wild with celebrations. The ban on alcohol was ignored. The war was over.[35]

While Legion membership had grown steadily in the years after WWI, the Second World War created an entire generation of men who were now eligible to join.

---

[35] Atwood, 2012

VETERAN'S VILLAGE

At the end of World War II, over 6000 new members were initiated into the Legion in one day, during the first (national) convention after the war. The Legion celebrated over a dozen Medal of Honor recipients and fed 50,000 veterans at the same convention.[36]

It was a boom time for the Legion. There were countless new members but there were also the same number of problems. While the country was better prepared for returning Veterans than after WWI, there were many issues to deal with on the personal, local and the national level.

Many men came back to unemployment and ended up at their American Legion post in general, and too many times the bar specifically. Post leaders published, *Veterans Betrayed*, a pamphlet describing the acute shortages of medical care, housing, transportation and other aid for Veterans and the failure of federal agencies to cope with the growing Veteran population.

At the end of WWII, Veteran families, families that had a blood or spousal relation to a Veteran numbered over 46,000,000 or 32 percent of the population. The end of the war brought tens of thousands of Veterans and their families to South Florida.

Miami-Dade County's population almost doubled from 1940 to 1950.

The post had over 6600 members in 1946.

Shortly after World War II, the Harvey Seeds post worked with the

---

[36] Legionnaire, 1945

Florida Highway Patrol to form the FHP auxiliary. Owen Bender, Vice Commander of Post 29 was the captain of the auxiliary in Dade County up until his death in 1965.[37]

The post was always open to the boys...if the boys were looking for a place where libations were a little harder, there was the post's restaurant-bar. [38]

The post has grown so fast that they asked the city to lend them the regular election voting machines in order to conduct post elections.

So many showed up so quickly that there was an acute shortage of housing. The post initiated the Dade County Veteran's Service Center. It tried to assist with housing, vocational training and disability claims, but could barely keep up with demand.

In 1946 members of the post came up with the Veteran's Village idea. The post, "tried to address the housing shortage for military families by re-opening World War II buildings on Miami Army air field, today's Miami International Airport. For $20 a month, families got wooden huts, 16 feet by 16 feet, with no running water or cooking facilities. Latrines could be 100 yards away. When newspapers complained about conditions, the Legion tried to shut the village but there was nowhere for Veterans to go. Holdouts were evicted into the streets, where they lived for days until space was found in Miami Springs town hall, private homes

---

[37] William Wilbanks, *Forgotten Heroes: Police Officers Killed in Dade County, 1895-1995*. Paducah, (Kentucky: Turner Publishing, 1996)

[38] Stella Suberman, *The GI Bill Boys: A Memoir*, (Knoxville: University of Tennessee Press, 2012)

and, ultimately, a migrant labor camp in Homestead."[39]

In a final move to address the issue, the executive committee of the post voted to try to secure FHA funding for Veteran housing, which would be built in what is now Legion Park. They had plans drawn up for 189 units but the general membership voted against the $1.4M loan obligation that would be necessary to assure completion.

P/C J.K. Williams began working on the draft commission.

With a housing shortage and not a lot of available work, Miami was not exactly a paradise for Veterans in 1946.

---

[39] Herald, 2016

BLACK VETERANS

World War One forever altered America's character. Fundamentally, the enduring legacy of this war [for us] lies in its commitment to the belief that all people, forging their identities, no matter how small their numbers, are entitled to the privilege of self-determination and to the principle that all people are created equal and are endowed with certain unalienable rights. The war gave Americans that new sense of their own national identity, one that emboldened them to help others realize theirs.[40]

Although they were one of the largest posts in the country, Harvey W Seeds was beholden to the same Jim Crow segregation that was still in place in other southern posts in the 1950's.

The American Legion had been very good about denouncing the Klu Klux Klan early on. The Klan was un-American and Fascist as far as the Legion was concerned and these two attributes were only slightly less offensive than Communism.

They had been less united about enforcing integration within its ranks, however. At the St Louis Caucus, in 1919, they proclaimed, "No color line, "but eschewed providing written guidance and instead allowed state departments to do as they wished.

The Army accepted a total of 13,024 African-American enlistees and 7 officers from Florida but the Legion wouldn't force integration after World War I.

---

[40] A Scott Berg, *World War I and America: Told By the Americans Who Lived It*, (Library of America, New York, NY, 2017)

Nowhere was the dichotomy of US segregation more glaring than in the wartime armed forces. Black troops were expected to support whole-heartedly the war effort to destroy fascism, yet abide by a system relegating them to an inferior position.[41]

World War II had helped position African Americans to achieve what they hadn't been able to in the past. Many African Americans were commissioned as and served admirably as aircraft pilots, allowing them into the officers' ranks, thereby showing the world that the barriers of segregation were unsubstantiated artifice.

Our Negro Veterans, published in 1947 described the segregated, 'pattern of community,' which sprouted after WWII. Social organizations, VFW, DAV and the Legion had a patchwork of policies, or in some cases, no official policy. The Louisiana Department of the Legion did not admit any Negroes before WWII. While segregation was not an official policy, the Texas Department was the first Legion organization to openly admit Negroes, while pointing them towards organizing separate posts from the main organization.

The largest black post (in the country at that time), in Louisville, Kentucky had 110 members, sponsored a Jazz orchestra and a Boy Scout troop. But most blacks had little enthusiasm for an organization that had no greater commitment to equality than American society as a whole.[42]

In Florida, Comrade H. Frost Bailey was elected Department Commander in 1946. During his tenure, Bailey announced the

---

[41] Atwood, 2012

[42] Pencak, 1989

integration of the *Colored Veterans of the World Wars* into the Florida Department as a separate district. There were 100 *Colored Veteran* posts state-wide and 32 auxiliary posts.

The post sent a letter endorsing Governor Fuller Warren's condemnation of the KKK. In what they believed to be a matter of fairness, they also petitioned the Miami City Council to, "appoint a negro judge to try negroes," in Miami. Although not an enlightened position, it was progressive for its time.

In 1960 the *40 & 8* split from the American Legion because they refused to allow blacks within their membership.

In the 1970's, the FBI would conduct counterintelligence operations against the Klan, which was still meeting in rural Miami and Ft Lauderdale. The Klan tried to hijack some of the key concepts of other organizations to legitimize themselves. They spoke of being anti-Communist and pro-Americanism.

The post wouldn't see its first black commander, James Colson, until 1993, almost 74 years after its inception.

OLD TIMERS

Edmond Gong, 17- year-old youth of Chinese ancestry, who was elected *President* by the 1947 Boys' Forum of National Government, sponsored by The American Legion, has joined the Miami Unit of the Florida National Guard here, as a private. Young Gong was elected *President* of the mock boys' United States Government set up by 100 selected lads from all over the nation who participated in the forum in Washington, D. C, August 1, to 8, 1947. Since his election young Gong has made numerous talks on behalf of Universal Military Training. He is now getting some training himself as a member of the 202nd Medical Detachment of the Florida National Guard here. He will graduate from Miami Senior High School next June. [43]

Gong was sent to Boys' State by Harvey W. Seeds.

From 1944 to 1948 the Harvey Seeds post spent over $150,000 in programs. That same year, Comrade E.F. Humer was elected National Sergeant-at-Arms as the national convention was held in Miami. While the post looked forward to that convention, they invested $80,000 in upgrades to the lounge and meeting areas of the *T House* building.

The Florida State Highway Department spent over $4,000,000 in improving roads leading into and around Miami where the 1948 national convention was held. They also installed over 4000 new bus benches.

---

[43] American Legion Wire Service, 1947

In the late 1940's the post accumulated multiple scrapbooks that documented post achievements that still survive to this day.

The 1947 Auxiliary sent 14 girls to Florida Girl's State.

The post property was ample, but one could sense that if an event were to somehow draw more than half of the 6,000 members the post had after WWII, the area would seem crowded.

Someone mentioned to post leadership that the deed for the property also included the island immediately east of the post in Biscayne Bay. Post leaders sought and successfully acquired a permit, allowing them to expand the small island. For the next 16 years plans were developed and discarded for everything from a beach to a boat house, but it was not to be.

Eventually the post went to the city council and was approved for development on the island, which was later squashed by the deal the post made to sell the park and obtain a sea wall.

The 1949 installation of all regional post officers was hosted by Harvey Seeds. About 1800 Legionnaires showed up for the events, the largest event of its kind to that date.

The post often shipped coconuts to Legion events to remind folks that the weather was usually better in Florida.. Photo courtesy post archives.

At the end of the decade, many founding members were reaching their 50's or later. Earle Edholm, first captain of the Drum Corps passed away. Past Commander William 'Bill' Green passed and was interred in the Legion plot at Woodlawn. Member names were showing up in the obituaries more than in newspaper headlines.

Two distinct factions emerged within the post, the young and the, 'old timers.' Membership had skyrocketed after World War II. Many Veterans ended up in Miami after the war and over 4000 joined the Harvey Seeds post alone. While these were exciting times, approximately 25% of the post consisted of, 'old timers'; Veterans who had served in World War I. The rest were World War II Veterans.

Later that year, Colonel Frank M. Williams, a founding member of the Legion presented the post with a copy of the original Paris caucus meeting notes, which were accepted as a gift by Commander Kelly.

U.S. Senator Estes Kefauver formed the Senate Crime Investigating Committee in 1949. He held a number of open hearings on the radio which riveted the American public as they exposed organized crime figures around the country.

Kefauver came to Miami and exposed an illegal gambling syndicate that had been entrenched in the community and counted a number of public officials on its payroll.

As a result of allegations of corruption, Dade County Sherriff, Jimmy Sullivan was forced out of office.

Midway through his fourth term as Post Commander, Thomas J Kelly resigned the position in order to serve as Sheriff of Dade County when the Governor asked him to replace Sullivan. Roby Wetmore, Past Vice-Commander, then became the first Veteran of only WWII to become Commander. Prior commanders had served in WWI or in both wars.

Kelly finished the previous Sheriff's term, then won election for another term. Under his leadership the police department opened its first crime lab and updated its capacities to include the latest investigative techniques. He consolidated and modernized all of the communications equipment. He also helped build a new headquarters and jail for the county.

Kelly's elections were mired in muck, however. During his first election, he had been accused of lying. He took a lie detector test and the resulting report got him in more trouble than if he would have just skipped the entire affair. He was vindicated but made a few enemies along the way.

When citizens voted to charter Metro –Dade County in 1957, Kelly's job became an appointed one. Kelly held the position with title of Safety Director, when he was fired by the City Manager in 1962. At the same time, Kelly had battled for his position to return to being an elected one. He won, but later lost the election of 1963 in another mudslinging contest.

Thomas J. Kelly was Sheriff for ten years. A plaque mounted on the wall outside the entrance of the old Dade County Public Safety Department Headquarters said, "In appreciation of his inspiring and untiring efforts to build an enduring and modern agency dedicated to law enforcement."

The Selective Service was activated in 1950 as conflict erupted on the Korean peninsula. Commander Wetmore read the descriptions of draft dodgers and deserters wanted by the FBI at post meetings.

KOREA

On July 28, 1950 near the road junction of Chinju and Hadong roads, Air Force SSG Edward A Lyon, member of the 6132nd Tactical Control Squadron, a veteran of World War II, became the first post member killed in Korea. He was killed by enemy snipers.

Trustee and Past Commander Thomas Kelly fervently urged the Legion and other fraternal organizations to combat subversiveness and Communism when he spoke at post meetings.

Past Commander Joe H Adams was elected National Vice-Commander 1950-1951. Post membership was over 4,700. Miami-Dade County population was only 495,000.

In the March 12, 1950 Constitutional Conference for the 10th District, the posts decided to support Captain Eddie Rickenbacker of the Eastern Airlines post as delegate to the national convention. Rickenbacker, a WWI ace and Medal of Honor recipient, kept a winter home in Coconut Grove.

The 1950 Tide of Toys collected nearly 50,000 toys for underprivileged children.

In 1950, Miami Herald columnist Jack Bell wrote a prescient column about the post. In it he cited the post's already burgeoning financial problems after the post failed to increase dues to $10 annually. "According to Commander Tom Kelly the post wound up 1949 with a $6000 deficit...the post donated 76 pints of blood (to the blood bank) and used 106. Why don't all those members participate? What are you waiting for - oil? The need is now, every day. And American Legion stands for service. Lease the darned stuff," he said, referring to the post's property.

On October 18, 1950, Hurricane King, a category 4 hurricane hit Miami with 135 mph winds. It was the strongest storm in almost 25 years and did over $10,000 damage to the post building.

In January of 1951 Legion membership was opened up to Korean War Veterans. Membership at the post hovered around 4700 at the time. Harvey Seeds was the sixth largest post in the country. Voting machines were borrowed from the city for post officer elections.

Past Commander Kelly noted to the general meeting that among the post's membership roll, there were two members of the city commission, two members of the county commission, a congressman and a United States Senator.

Throughout the 1950's the Legion was embroiled in American politics. National Commander Earl Cocke advocated for an American Foreign Legion that would be dedicated to fighting communist insurgencies around the world. Cocke was lauded as a war hero. He had been captured by the Germans in WWII and faced a firing squad. The bullets missed him and he dropped to the ground, left for dead.

On July 28 1951, a funeral service was held at the post home for Edward A Lyon, the first post member killed in the Korean War, on the anniversary of his death.

The National Convention came to Miami in 1951. As a way to assist police and upon the request of the Governor of Florida, Harvey Seeds stood up an Auxiliary Police detachment under the supervision of P/C James Barney. At one point the unit was called the Legion Reserve Police and later was renamed the State Highway Patrol auxiliary and was opened to other Legionnaires state-wide. The volunteers logged more than 33,000 hours of guard duty over the next few years at no cost to Florida taxpayers.

Through the 1950's programs included grants to the Foundation for Infantile Paralysis (Polio); the Veteran's Aid Fund and blood drives that were organized for the VA Hospital. Boys State in 1951 sent 24 boys to Tallahassee.

P/C Jack Cleary was an ardent advocate for an Infantile Paralysis (Polio) cure. Photo courtesy post archives.

The Americanism committee reported early in 1951 that they had helped celebrate the indoctrination of 75 new Americans to date with another ceremony scheduled for Memorial Day weekend, where 300 more Americans would pledge allegiance for the first time.

Early in 1952, the post helped distribute literature developed by B'nai B'rith called, "Freedom, Stalin Style." It detailed the Soviet merchandise that was being sold in America that indirectly supported Stalin. A task force of Legionnaires visited local businesses to spread the word. They were also looking for shop owners who might be complicit and therefore conducting what would be considered, "un-American activities."

The same year, the post hosted the U.S. Army Field Band. The band was on tour helping promote the military during a particularly trying time, as the Korean War was in full swing. Over 4000 people attended the concert and over 200 pledges were made for blood donation at the door of the free event.

The post brought over 10,000 coconuts to the 1952 national convention to remind everyone else how much nicer it was in Florida.

1952 saw one of the most successful, "Old-timers," reunions. Adjutant Jerry Ganz was so moved that he wrote about it in meeting minutes. The reunion, "gave the younger members a chance to meet see and hear the pioneers who founded and were responsible for the finest post in the American Legion...they came on crutches, in wheelchairs, on canes. Some did not show the ravages of the years gone by but each stood with pride and told the story of their origin with the American Legion...This night should not die. It should be perpetuated and made an annual feature of post activities. If old Soldiers must fade away, they should fade away on nights like this, in the companionship of comrades they met many years ago."[44]

740 guests were invited to the 4th of July party at the post property in 1953, including 167 children from the *Children's Home*. The event included horse and carnival rides as well as

---

[44] Harvey Seeds general membership meeting minutes, 1952

musical performances from bands including the drum corps. The number was eclipsed the following year as 842 paid admissions were sold to the New Year's party. The proceeds were used dutifully as 23 boys were sent to Boys State.

Over 50 post members passed away between 1952 and 1953. The surviving founding members of the post were still in their 50's or 60's. World War II Veterans were in their 30's and 40's and a new wave of Korean-era Veterans were just starting to join.

81 Miami-Dade County Veterans made the ultimate sacrifice during the Korean War.

AMERICANISM

1956 brought the recognition of three generations of the same family as members of the post: Robert Lee Stephens was a charter member of the post. His son, Ed Barker joined in 1926 and Jack Barke, Ed's son, joined in 1949.

President Eisenhower declared that September 16, 1954 was *Citizenship Day*. The post held an event where almost 1000 new U.S. citizens were sworn in. Later that year, on Veteran's Day, 451 more citizens were sworn in.

The American Legion National Convention came to Miami again in 1955. That year the post sent 19 boys to Boys State and sent the drum corps to march in Havana's *Mardi Gras* parade and festival.

Bartenders stand ready around the famous Harvey Seeds bar. The photo was undated but probably from the 1951 or 1955 conference. Artist Robert Bruce painted most of the murals depicting Florida history. Photo courtesy post archives.

A new organization, the *Twenty and Eight*, meaning twenty women and eight jeeps was formed from within the active female Legionnaires.

The Legion locked horns with legislators that year. At the 1956 department convention, Legionnaires unanimously agreed to protest against the Bradley commission as it endangered Veteran's benefits for non-service related illnesses or disabilities.

Roughly 7.8 million Veterans had used the G.I. Bill education benefits by 1956, about 2.2 million to attend colleges or universities and an additional 5.6 million for some kind of training program.

The Legion was reaping the benefits of the multitude of Americans who had been in uniform at one time or another, if not as members, then at least as like-minded advocates. Almost 60 U.S. Senators and almost 300 U.S. Representatives were Veterans at this time in American history. The numbers would actually peak right after Vietnam. Locally, Dante Fascell, a former drum corps member was in the Florida House. P/C Tom Kelly was county sheriff, Dan Aitchison, Miami Herald City Editor was a Legionnaire.

Comrade Richard E Gerstein was elected as Florida's State Attorney, the youngest person to hold that post to that date.

Kay Smiley Thurston was installed as the post's first female Vice Commander in 1960.

That year saw Miami gain the immense gravity and focus of international attention, which would last for several years. The forty-second Annual Convention came to Miami Beach on October 17-20, 1960. The convention began with a notable six hour parade through Miami. Legionnaires reviewed American rockets at Cape Canaveral and later military fortifications and aircraft in the area. Presidential contenders Richard Nixon and John F Kennedy visited Florida and spoke at the convention, seeking votes in the upcoming election.

In 1961, geography again put Miami in the spotlight as members of Cuban Veterans of United States Armed Forces Post 286, American Legion, conducted memorial services for Howard Anderson, Past Commander of Havana Post 1, American Legion. Anderson was executed by the Castro government without a trial.

Massed colors of the Department of Florida and nearly 100 American Legion posts fluttered in the sunshine as Taps were sounded by the Harvey Seeds Drum and Bugle Corp.

In his memorial address, Commander Burke asserted that the death of Howard Anderson "reiterates for us why... the elimination of a Soviet bastion 90 miles from the shores of the United States must be achieved by whatever means necessary — sanctions, embargoes or military action."[45]

A time capsule was found during construction under the post portico in 1962. It was buried by Past Commander Sam McCahill in 1934. It contained a copy of the post property title and newspaper clippings of Legion achievements from the early 30's.

The post was roiled in the same controversies and schisms as the rest of the country during the 1960's. Resolutions seemed to be formed at every meeting regarding one political or social event or another.

---

[45] Legion, American Legion Magazine 1961

In mid-1962 a group of Cubans attended the post meeting and requested the Legion's help in putting together a fighting force to take back Cuba from Castro. The failed Bay of Pigs Invasion in 1961 was still fresh in their minds.

Post leaders quickly put together a memorandum for local police as well as the FBI.

A June 1962 copy of Legionnaire noted that the post was sending two, "Latin-American young men," to Boys State for the first time in order to, "learn in detail how democracy is made to work."

P/C Bill Davis signed the charter for the Sons of the American Legion Squadron #29 on April 2, 1963. A dozen young men were on the initial charter. The Sons had previously held a charter and even enough membership for their own, junior drum corps in the 30's and 40's but had dissolved after World War II.

In an ardent editorial, the January 22, 1963 issue of the Legionnaire said, "The Adjutant was instructed to notify official Washington of our deep concern about the handling of the Bay of Pigs invaders. The post members want to know why 23 American political prisoners are still held in Cuba….We are glad that refugee Cubans can find freedom here…we must remind Washington that the old saying, 'charity begins at home,' is still valid."

In November 1964 the post signaled it was with Director of FBI J Edgar Hoover and against Reverend Martin Luther King Jr. In 1965 the post protested singer Pete Seeger's appearance in Miami. Seeger was indicted for contempt of Congress during the McCarthy era. In May of 1965 the post proclaimed its support of President Johnson against the Dominican Republic. The post also petitioned the VA for a Veteran's cemetery in North Miami.

Political commentary, inclinations and petitions would turn to action, protests and even violence in the following years.

VIETNAM

Hurricane Cleo hit Miami in 1964. The post's Civil Defense team mustered and they shuttled needy people to shelters. They secured the facility and waited out the storm in the building. The storm damaged the old building and this was a final straw for those people who wanted to demolish the grand *Tea House* and build a new structure. The minority grew more vocal and even gained support.

By May of 1965 the Harvey W. Seeds Sons of the American Legion chapter was at risk of losing its charter as fewer than a dozen members were active.

Good luck, it seems, has always walked alongside Harvey Seeds members, as Robert C. Hahn, one of the few active members, won a 1965 convertible Ford at a contest during the national convention.

It was evident to senior Legion officials early on that the war in Vietnam was not being executed in an efficient manner. Legion officials had direct communication with senior military leaders and they realized that there was a disconnect between what the military was telling them and what policies were then developed by politicians and furthermore what was being released to the public.

Second-guessing the government's policy was not condoned. [46]

---

[46] Thomas A Rumer, *The American Legion, An Official History*, (New York, M. Evans and Co, 1990)

In March of 1966 a lengthy and well-publicized post resolution called Cassius Clay, "unpatriotic, bombastic and crass, "as he avoided the Vietnam draft. Several other Legion posts joined in the resolution to censor Clay.

Comrade Hazel Allen was elected Florida Department's Historian for 1966. The post tried to arrange to send 5,000 books to the Soldiers and Marines in Vietnam. The Guard of Honor was re-organized under the District in order to share some of the costs. A per-capita, 'tax' of 10 cents per member was collected and donated to the group

In 1967 a rash of *mob-style* hits killed four suspected criminals. Miami, however, had not previously experienced this type of criminal uneasiness.

Comrade Cameron Craig, Charter Member and Historian during 1967-1968 assembled a comprehensive yearbook that survived mostly intact. While this yearbook relied heavily on *The Miami Legionnaire* and Feibelman's *History of Harvey W. Seeds* for its narrative portions, it also included a compilation of insightful data such as *40 & 8* statistics, a listing of Past Commanders and other elected offices held, Life Members and members who joined prior to 1950. The yearbook also holds the last photos of the T-House before most of it was demolished.

One of the last photos as parts of the old T House were demolished. Photo courtesy post archives.

Groundbreaking for the new post HQ featured a visit by Congressman, Claude Pepper. Photo courtesy post archives.

The *T House* and 37 acres were sold to the City of Miami for over $800,000 and turned into a park and public building.

The city obtained financing from the government, which also threw in money for a sea wall, which keeps Biscayne Bay from washing away any more of the Legion or city property during storms.

Most of the *T House* building was demolished.

Old and new buildings can be seen in a wide shot from what is now Legion Park. Photo courtesy post archives.

"All that remains today of William Ogden's original 12 bedroom Tee House Plantation residence is American Legion Park's two-story 5000 square foot Community Center, one of the few examples of George Pfeiffer's work to survive in Miami. "[47]

---

[47] Robert Flanders, *AL Harvey W. Seeds Post #29*, Biscyane Times, 2004

The bulk of the money from the sale went into the construction of the new post home.

On May 20, 1967 the post dedicated its $400,000, "showplace of the entire Southern Legion." [48] It featured banquet facilities, an auditorium, both auxiliary and trophy rooms as well as a recreation room and a large cocktail lounge which featured a stage with a large window that overlooked Biscayne Bay.

Demolishing the building was important both symbolically and financially. The post gave up the last big tract of private land that ran from Biscayne Bay to Biscayne Boulevard. The post was able to put some money away from the sale of the land and position itself for the tumult that was coming as membership began to dwindle from its height in 1946.

---

[48] Georgia Lyons, *Harvey Seeds History Scrapbook,* (Miami, 1978)

An early photo of the new behemoth, built in the brutal design style popular at the time. Photo courtesy post archives.

From April 1967 to April 1968, over 104 post members pass away. The post sent 10 young men to *Boys State* that year. Proceeds from the weekly bingo games went to purchase care packages for service members in Vietnam.

The Legions position was, at the beginning of the Vietnam conflict, a pro-American, anti-communist drumbeat.

The American Legion's National Foreign Relations Committee was vocal about American engagements in Vietnam. While calls for action and reaction to North Korean aggression were common in those days, in 1965 National Commander Johnson warned against another Korea-like stalemate.

Auxiliary members gather to lay a wreath on Memorial Day, 1967. Photo courtesy post archives.

1968 was a socio-political firestorm in American history. The unexpected *Tet Offensive* in North Vietnam showed Americans that the war was definitely not under control. Walter Cronkite said it out loud for the first time on CBS News that year. Over 16,000 American servicemen were killed in Vietnam in 1968 alone.

Martin Luther King Jr was assassinated in April. Lyndon Johnson dropped out of the presidential election. Robert Kennedy was shot and killed in June. Richard Nixon became President.

A race riot was met with police violence which killed three African American men, injured a baby and saw a Florida Highway Patrol armored truck drive down Miami's neighborhood streets shooting tear gas, apparently arbitrarily, into homes.

As Vietnam dragged on, national headquarters shifted their emphasis from an ardent call for the extermination of Communism to the well-being of and rehabilitation of Veterans returning from war and their reintegration to society. By 1968 the Legion declared that victory seemed an impossibility and that they deplored the loss of life of American combatants. [49]

First Vice Commander, Paul J. Oneill resigned in September of 1969 and took a position in the Subversive Activities Control Board under President Nixon.

The post had 58 Life Members at this time.

Throughout the 60's and 70's the *40 & 8* gave away thousands of dollars in scholarship money to nursing students at Jackson Memorial Hospital. Some of those students kept in touch with the *40 & 8* and wrote letters to the post about their progress.

On April 8, 1971, Charles F. Thomas IV was a company commander in Vietnam. Thomas made the ultimate sacrifice as an American Soldier. He died of wounds suffered in a mortar attack in Binh Dinh, Vietnam. American Legion Post #117 in Palm Bay is named in his honor.

---

[49] Rumer, 1990

HARVEY W. SEEDS

On 31 December, 1972, the Miami Herald published a roll of the South Floridians killed or missing in Vietnam. Photo courtesy archive.

Comrade Johnson E. Davis, won election as Department Commander in 1971. Later he became National Executive Committee member and positioned himself to run for National Commander in 1979.

1972 was tumultuous in national politics and domestic affairs as well. The national leadership of the Legion floated a resolution to give amnesty to draft dodgers during the annual convention. This brought much dissent among the Legion rank and file. Locally, Harvey Seeds saw a flair in racism and reverse racism, where members voted resolutions up and down based on the color of the skin of the person who made the motion.

After living in Miami for 67 years, Past Commander R.V. Waters retired to Stuart, Florida.

In May of 1972, Miami Beach Post #85 tried to recognize Miami Beach 9th grader, Alfred Kohn with an award for scholarship and service. Kohn refused the award, giving the Legion a dose of its own activism. He called the Legions, "conservative stance...abhorrent." In another low point in Legion public relations, Post #85's commander compared the 9th grader to a long-haired hippie who had, "no regard for our country." [50]

By January of 1973 the American Legion had over 2.7 million members nation-wide. The post had over 1100 paid members but committees were not able to meet the quorum requirements in the by-laws and the mechanisms for regular operations began to suffer. By-laws were amended to reflect only 50 members needed to be present to amend by-laws and enact other regulations, where prior to 1973, 100 members needed to be

---

[50] J. Anthony Lukas, "Report from Convention City, " *NY Times*. (July 9, 1972)

present.

As Vietnam and the draft subsided, over 50,000 Soldiers were becoming Veterans monthly nation-wide and the Legion was positioning itself to provide Service Officers and support for those who might not know all of the benefits they were entitled to. Only about 30 of the post members were Vietnam Veterans at this time.

At the same time the Legion made its position clear to government; they voted unanimously against a blanket amnesty for draft dodgers. Outgoing National Commander Robert Eaton predicted, incorrectly, that the new professional Army would return to a draft system within a few years.

The Legion had worked through the 1960's and 1970's to maintain its role as what Historian Thomas Rumer describes as a," patriotic touchstone."

Locally, the post expanded the headquarters building, adding a second stage and ballroom.

Any dissent from full-throated support for American aims were, well, un-American. As military objectives gave way to political goals, however, and multiple presidential administrations fumbled with a solution for peace, the Legion too had to evolve.

The country sank into a severe recession that lasted until 1975.

SPIRIT OF '76

Election drama is not restricted to federal political contests in America. In 1978, Executive Committee member John Henry Phillip Von Hagen attempted to get his name closer to the top of the ballot in an upcoming Harvey Seeds election. He wanted to run as, 'Hagen'. He had convinced the Commander to agree but the Election Committee noted that the member had never used only 'Hagen' and all of his official documents had his last name as 'Von Hagen, so the Commander's decision was overturned.

Undaunted, Von Hagen began a smear campaign against his rivals, sending fake post bulletins to some members in an attempt to discredit his rivals. Von Hagen was caught using the post's stamp machine without permission and the counterfeit flyers were discovered. He was suspended from the post for the year.

He came back and won election as post Historian for 1979 and 1980. Finally, in 1981, he was found guilty of assaulting another Legionnaire and asked to turn in his membership card.

He was reinstated in 1983.

The post joined with groups such as *Daughters of the American Revolution* to celebrate the American bicentennial in 1976.

On March 18, 1977, the indefatigable work of Past Commander Robert H Wheeler came to fruition. The post installed a monument for all branches of the military and to all who gave their lives in defense of liberty. The same year, the post won 2nd place in the National history contest for a scrapbook put together by Comrade Georgia Lyons. In it she noted that from May 1977 to April 1978, over 65 members pass away.

The Veteran's monument at the post, was erected in 1977. Photo by author.

One notable member who passed during those days was Harry

Acker. Acker was a machine shop owner. He had been a Miami resident since 1913. He was drafted in WWI. He was 40 & 8 *Chef de Gare* and was named Honorary Commander of the post in 1976. He was the longest living charter member of Harvey Seeds Post #29, going to his reward on February 22, 1978.

The post-Vietnam era was replete with clashes between conservative culture and the disco generation at the local and national levels.

Grudgingly, weekly disco dances began at the post in 1979. There was a $2 cover charge.

Executive committee meetings seemed to focus around one emergency after another. Most of the problems occurred in or because of the bar. In 1976, the post paid one patron's medical bills after she slipped and fell in the bar. They suspended a drunken member for life after he struck an office staff member. They sanctioned members for breaking furniture, burning holes in couches and a myriad of other excesses.

 Bar tenders skimmed from the register. Member's bar privileges were suspended at almost every executive committee meeting.

The position of Lounge Manager may as well have been posted on the post stationary and elected because he was called into every meeting to account for one thing or another. The job itself seemed like a revolving door with turnover at Lounge Manager an almost yearly event.

John Delserro wrote a letter to the executive committee, after having been caught running a cash card game at the bar. He asked for forgiveness and for reinstatement of his lounge privileges but was suspended from the lounge for six months.

The long list of suspended, admonished and barred members garnered a few unexpected names. In 1978, Legion values were not yet in step with liberal society and long-time Sergeant-at-Arms, Tony Perdomo had his lounge privileges suspended for using profanity in the lounge area.

Apparently, cursing, was considered as great a crime as assault in the 70's. Legionnaire Dennis Collins pulled a knife on another patron at the bar. He was only suspended for a year.

That same year the post revenue took a hit as legalized gambling was on the ballot for Miami-Dade County but the measure lost. The backlash was a crackdown on all gambling that forced the regular post bingo games to shut down. That revenue stream to the operational fund was critical to post survival and things spiraled downwards from that point.

In another blow, the City of Miami closed the post bar for a while for lack of proper insurance and other paperwork issues. It was a tough year.

By 1979 over 100 members were dying every year. The post couldn't afford the fireworks for its 4th of July picnic for the first time in its 80 year history.

Past Historian, Hortense Photos was appointed as co-editor of the Miami Legionnaire by the Executive Committee in 1980. In one of her first reports she noted, ironically, that history books were not being properly kept at the post home.

Though fewer in numbers, Legionnaire patriotism hadn't diminished. Post members circulated a petition to try and convince the government to place the battleship Missouri at the Port of Miami in perpetuity.

Ironically the *Mighty Mo* was taken out of retirement and reactivated in 1984. She served in the Persian Gulf before retiring to Pearl Harbor.

In the 70's the WWII generation began to retire and post members trickled away to retirement communities along Florida's Gulf Coast and basically anywhere away from the big cities where retirement checks wouldn't go very far.

The composition of the membership was changing and the Vietnam Veterans were earning their way into the executive positions of the post. As only 249 of the 2800 members voted in 1979's post election, the WWII Veterans lost the majority of the committee seats and the Korean and Vietnam Veteran generation officially took over.

Miami Mayor Stephen Clark, mindful of the post's strong political history, addressed the post membership on a number of occasions.

"You can, I don't know, just feel the patriotism her," Comrade Tom Dempsey told a Miami Herald reporter about Harvey's By the Bay. "This is just like any other bar, except when you walk through that door, you feel comradeship."

RUSSIANS

The Soviets invaded Afghanistan, ratcheting up tension between the Superpowers and escalating the *Cold War*. The *Oil Crisis* of 1979 shocked people into financial worries and perhaps tilted some towards voting against incumbent Jimmy Carter, who was blamed for a number of calamities, national and international. The Iranian Hostage Crisis started in 1979 and didn't end until the day he left office.

Regardless of how people felt, the Selective Service system was reactivated in 1979 and young men over the age of 18 had to register again. Mindful of the criticisms of the past, where minorities and the poor bore the brunt of draft boards for Vietnam, there were no educational deferments going forward. The Legion kept its members informed of the new policies.

A number of Legionnaires were appointed to run their local Selective Service Boards. They were the first line of defense against another unjust draft.

While the Legion and the nation looked ahead to rebuilding the military, they were constantly occupied with all the new benefits issues stemming from Vietnam. Agent Orange, a defoliant used by the U.S. and later found to cause Cancer, sprouted congressional hearings, lawsuits and thousands of Veteran's benefits claims.

The Legion was at the tip of the proverbial benefits spear, calling on Congress to release information, demanding research on the issue and demanding care for sick Veterans.

As Thomas Rumer wrote in, *An Official History 1919-1989*, the, "spectral influence of the founders of the Legion in 1919 was apparent (in the 1980s)." The Legion set forth resolutions that, "promoted World War I –era Americanism along with a foreign policy and a national security stance tailored now to a troubled nuclear age."

Some Veterans became disaffected by Selective Service, by society, by government conflict. A September 2, 1980 article in the Miami Herald quoted a Vietnam Veteran, "I want to forget all that. I disliked most of the people in the Army and I figure the Legion is where they all wound up."

Arthur McDuffie, a former Marine, died from injuries sustained at the hands of four white police officers trying to arrest him after a high-speed chase in December of 1979. The officers were tried and acquitted for manslaughter and evidence tampering, among other charges.

The Miami Herald devoted many columns of print to trying to understand the causes of that year's race riots. As if the social injustices of segregation and racism (displayed overtly by the murder of McDuffie) weren't enough, Miami's African Americans had the added disadvantage of competing with the newly arrived Cubans for limited resources.

One study, published by the Herald, showed that in 1960, 25% of gas stations in Miami were owned by blacks. By 1980 that number was 9% and the Hispanic-owned number was 48%. [51]

The Dade County Elections Department, which annually loaned Harvey Seeds voting machines, changed their policies and requested payment to use the county's machines. The post quit

---

[51] Miami Herald, (May 17, 1981), 4E

using the machines and went back to paper ballots.

The post bar was disruptive to post operations from the inside out as well as from the outside in. In a meeting at the post home on June 26, Commander Old reminded all members of the Executive Committee that they were not to come to the meeting under the influence.

If they did, they would be asked to leave and marked absent.

Regardless, the bar remained active as it brought in a regular income to the post and on special events the post could count on a few thousand dollars in liquor sales to bolster lagging membership dues.

A number of shake-ups changed the organization in these years. A lawsuit against the post diminished the coffers by $75,000. Commander McGrath initiated changes in the by-laws after a number of Executive Committee members were unable to execute the responsibilities of their positions and as dwindling numbers of members came to meetings.

By Veteran's Day, 1981, only five WWII Veterans were active in the post. Next door at Legion Park, as many as 50 people would huddle around the old Legion building looking for shelter nightly.

P/C Joe Friedman warned the members that they had a responsibility to run for elected offices, as attendance dwindled.

Wednesday night dart tournaments kept a few people coming back on a regular basis and the post hosted state-level dart competitions on a number of occasions in the 1980's.

The post participated in the nation-wide drive to fund the restoration of the Statue of Liberty in New York. They also continued ardent support of Americanism activities, participating in a naturalization ceremony almost every year, which saw thousands of new American citizens sworn in.

At the 67th annual National Convention in New Orleans in 1985, resolution #288 called for designating a POW/MIA Empty Chair at all official meetings of The American Legion as a physical symbol of the thousands of American POW/MIAs still unaccounted for from all wars and conflicts involving the United States. The 8th District of the AL Department of Missouri posted on their FB page, "..... a reminder for all of us to spare no effort to secure the release of any American prisoners from captivity, the repatriation of the remains of those who died bravely in defense of liberty, and a full accounting of those missing.'

After many years of Legion service, culminating in Post Commander duties 1985-1986, Gordon Fenwick and his wife Eleanor retired to New Port Richey, Fl.

William Wolff was born in 1921 in New Jersey. His father had been a WWI and a Mexican border Veteran so Wolff lied about his age and joined the New Jersey National Guard at age 15. A child of the Depression, he balanced finishing school, work and attending National Guard drill until he was mobilized in WWII.

Wolff survived a ship sinking during the war and met Anna Walters after the war. Anna was herself a Veteran. She had been a Navy WAVE and worked in Washington D.C. in communications and intelligence.

The Wolffs moved to Miami in the 1950's but became involved in the post after retiring in the 1980's. Bill became an executive committee member and Anna, known as "Nan," served in a number of positions culminating in her becoming the first female post commander in 1991.

During 1986-1987 two Scouts from Troop 29 were sponsored for Eagle Scout rank.

On June 7, 1988, Frank Reese of Post #199 in West Palm Beach became the first African-American Florida Department Commander.

In 1989 the post petitioned for and the City of Miami agreed to name the street between Biscayne Boulevard and Biscayne Bay, at NW 64th Street, *American Legion Way*. 7th Avenue south from Legion Park was re-designated *Legion Park Drive*.

In June 1989, a long-time member and advocate for the post, Congressman, Claude D Pepper died. Pepper was a supporter of many of the post's activities and his presence provided a legitimacy to some of the post's endeavors that would not have been available otherwise. His correspondence can be found constantly among the post committee and commander's correspondence. He was always in favor of helping Veteran's causes.

He was awarded the Presidential Medal of Freedom by President Bush before his death.

BLIGHT

"In its early years Legion Park flourished, but by the late 1980's the park had become a haven for large numbers of homeless people, turning it into the worst possible urban nightmare. Repeated attempts by the city to remove the homeless were rebuffed by Federal Judge C. Clyde Atkins, who forbade removal of the homeless until the city had an alternative plan to house and care for them." [52]

In the 70's and 80's, Miami began to grow farther west. The corridors east of I-95 were mostly ignored by developers who were looking for land and space to build malls. The older parts of the city, including almost everything around the post, fell into disrepair and urban blight.

Director of Legion Park, Harry McFarlane, told the Miami Herald, "In 1980, we ended up canceling a lot of our programs at night because people were afraid to come here. It was dangerous. I got mugged myself."

Removal of the homeless was finally accomplished in 1994, but the damage was done, local residents had stopped using the park and it fell into disrepair, all but ignored by a city now overwhelmed by corruption and financial problems. The only bright spot in the park was a program sponsored by Douglas Gardens, the Jewish Home for the Aged, who used the parks building as a senior center. But in 1995
the senior center was moved into the American Legion next door." [53]

Nationally, the Legion found itself advocating against a new

---

[52] Flanders, *Miami's Legion Park*, 2003

[53] Flanders, *Miami's Legion Park*, 2003

enemy. A Supreme Court decision, *Texas v. Johnson*, where the court decided that burning the flag was not illegal, as had been the law in 48 of 50 states previously, infuriated the Legion. For many years the American Legion had been a harbinger of respect for everything flag-related. It published Flag Code pamphlets and educated posts, members and anyone who would listen on flag etiquette.

The American Legion as an organization found itself in staunch defiance of the status quo. As a response, they quickly gathered over a million signatures on a petition to protect the flag against public burning and presented it to Congress. Impressed by the Legion's power to organize such a massive response, Congress amended the Flag Protection Act of 1968 to protect against desecration of the flag. Once again, however, the Supreme Court found that, "the government's interest in preserving the flag as a symbol does not outweigh the individual's First Amendment right to disparage that symbol through expressive conduct."

In defiance of the Supreme Court, the American Legion has actively petitioned Congress since 1990 for a Constitutional Amendment to protect the flag.

Forever faithful to the memories of our past, on September 16, 1990 the Auxiliary, along with other chapters throughout the country held a bell ringing ceremony to commemorate the historic signing of the Constitution of the United States.

The first Gulf War began in 1990 and created a new generation of Veterans.

Harvey W. Seeds did not have an African American commander until P/C James Colson Jr. took over for Anna, "Nan" Wolff, the post's first female commander. She passed to her reward while still in office, in her third elected term, in 1993.

In 1995, The Miami Herald interviewed Commander Nick Williams for their Memorial Day edition. He said, "The ceremonies have been getting smaller and smaller. We lose veterans every year. People are not as patriotic as they used to be."

At the time the post had eight surviving WWI Veterans in its ranks.

Senator Bob Graham came to the post in 1992 to helped honor Vietnam Veterans who had never received their commendation medals.

With membership aging and dwindling, the post rented space out within the building to other organizations. At one point the 'Save Dade," foundation had an office in the building. A Jewish day-care for the elderly rented space downstairs. The Cosmopolitan Community Center, a gay rights group had an office in the building.

Harvey Seeds was not the only post suffering and it least it maintained its heritage. A Miami Herald article noted, "The posts are places where veterans can meet and exchange stories. But, as older war veterans die, many posts have lost their histories.

They have no written records -- and neither does the state or national office -- telling about the posts' namesakes."

"It's a hole in our heritage,"(Roz)Mullen (of the Florida department of the American Legion) said. "When we lose that knowledge, we lose part of who we are. It's very important to know where our beginnings are and why you're there." [54]

---

[54] C.I. Moss, 2 Dade posts trying to recover history, *Miami Herald*, (May 28, 1995) KE2

Dante Fascell moved to Florida in 1925 when his Italian-immigrant parents bought a business in South Miami. As a kid, he was in the Greater Miami Boys Drum and Bugle Corps. He accompanied Jean McNamee, Cesar La Monaca's daughter, to prom.

He later joined the Florida National Guard and served in the Italian and North African campaigns. Upon his return, he jumped into Florida politics, helping create Biscayne National Park, and co-creating the *War Powers Act*. He was a tireless advocate for Veterans. In 1998, Congressman Dante Fascell went on to his reward.

"The Legion, born in the aftermath of a world conflict, reinforced by World War II and the Korean War, turned its energies to the endless battles of peace – against apathy, social decay, delinquency, the neglect of those who are in need and forgetfulness of national ideals." [55]

The post was on a moderate upswing financially around 2000, until Larry McGrath became commander. Under his leadership the post, "lost a lot of money under him. He put us in a bad spot."[56]

On the morning of September 11, 2001, a series of coordinated terrorist attacks killed 2,996 people on American soil.

The actions of the U.S. government in the ensuing months have had reverberating consequences seventeen years later and will be etched in history as the beginning of the *War on Terror*.

---

[55] William Pencak, *For God and Country*, (Boston, Northeastern University Press,1989)

[56] Interview, L.A. Walden, July 5, 2018

The world lost the simple, brutal paradigm of conventional warfare. From that point forward, civilians were targets in the conflict. Overseas and at home, security became a constant concern.

U.S. Citizenship and Immigration Services, formerly Immigration and Naturalization Services, leased office space in the post's auditorium in 2003, extending a needed lifeline to a failing post. The lease lasted five years. The relationship was a symbiotic one while it lasted as Harvey Seeds has historically supported naturalization efforts through its Americanism program.

On Veteran's Day 2004, Past Commander Robert Flanders published American Legion Harvey W. Seeds Post #29, 85 Years of Miami History in the Biscayne Boulevard Times. Flanders was an advocate for the post and the Biscayne corridor area. He tried to inform the neighbors of the good Harvey Seeds could do in the community.

Flanders fought against the development that would eventually consume the post building and property.

By 2005 the *new post* building was almost 40 years old. The bar was dilapidated and fewer and fewer Veterans were showing up for meetings and even for beers. Post leaders decided that an upgrade to the bar would improve business and therefore improve income. The bar was closed for eight months and the leadership spent more than $100,000 in renovations in the bar, alone.

"We spent over $200,000 updating the bar and other parts of the building, said Past Commander Al Underwood. "It was ridiculous."

The investment never paid off but it did bring an upswing in media attention to the post.

Writer John Colagrande Jr. memorialized it in a feature he wrote for the Miami Herald:

> ``This place is neat,'' says the kid, following his grandfather into the lounge, a beautiful bar and restaurant with a retro feel, located in the rear of the building. The walls are covered in vintage WWII- and Vietnam-era posters and memorabilia - Uncle Sam reminding us to buy war bonds, a woman urging other women to enlist in the Navy Waves, a simple black flag remembering the POW's.
>
> The grandson wants to play, but can't decide between darts, pool, and the piano. He walks over to the jukebox.
>
> ``Who's Artie Shaw?'' he asks no one in particular, before considering taking his chances on the Pamela Anderson
>
> ``Barb Wire'' pinball machine. He finally settles into the old, worn couch in front of the big-screen television.
>
> A couple of patrons sit at the long bar, sipping on drinks. The vet joins them. ``How's it going?'' asks the bartender.
>
> ``Damn good,'' says the vet, ordering a Jack and Coke.
>
> ``Coming to the barbecue on the Fourth?'' asks one of the patrons. ``Should be a nice firework display at Legionnaire Park, on account of the war and all.''
>
> ``Wouldn't miss it for the world,'' says the vet, staring out the back window, where an old cannon rests on the grass, defending Biscayne Bay from invasion, teens fly by on wave runners, and people fish off the rocks.

``Wouldn't miss it for the world."[57]

The 2007 Veteran's Day event was cited as the, "most successful," in a number of years according to meeting minutes. Congresswoman Ileana Ros-Lehtinen spoke and City Mayor and commissioners were in attendance.

Korean War Veteran and Commander at the time, Philip Johnson, said he hoped the lounge's sleeker look and improved restaurant would draw in not just more drinkers and diners, but new members from the surrounding community.

"The entire facility was in poor shape and turned a lot of people off," he said to the Miami Herald.. "We wanted to provide a place where people could come with their families. People thought of this place as a bar where some old guys got together to smoke, drink and talk about their days in the service."

The Post-9/11 G.I. Bill, an update to the original legislation fostered by the Legion was passed into law in 2008. It provided enhanced benefits for Veterans serving after September 10, 2001, including a benefit transfer option, which allows Veterans who do not use all of their educational benefits to transfer them to spouses or children.

Students and faculty from the University of Detroit Mercy School of Law came to South Florida with "Project Salute," a tour that was part of a Veterans law course at the school in 2008. They provided free legal information and assistance on federal benefits issues to low-income veterans at Harvey Seeds, among other places.

In the September 2009 issue of the *American Legion Magazine*,

---

[57] John Colagrande, *The Great American Bar*, Miami Herald, (July 2, 2004), p. 56MS.

National Commander, David K. Rehbein reflected on the Legion's responsibility to represent, "homefront support," to the thousands of duty-driven professionals in the military serving in the *War on Terror*.

"Legion Park has been reborn, an asset for the whole Upper Eastside, its future secured by residents who treasure it as a beautiful oak tree filled catalyst for the neighborhood, with space for community and homeowner meetings, a summer camp for children, and the host for special events such as Halloween and the 4th of July." [58]

With membership and financial resources in decline, the post was unable to react quickly when vandals painted and cut the hands off of the Woodlawn monument. Luckily, Felix Sosa-Camejo members, Post #346 organized and with the help of a Florida International University sculptor, put the statues back in shape.

In 2009 the post held events, , like "Rock and Remember," a concert and fund-raiser, to try and keep itself financially afloat, but as the area was revitalized and a farmer's market came to the park each weekend, and sports were organized at the park, it seemed that the brutalist building next door was more and more out of place than ever.

Robert Holcomb was, by many accounts, a Renaissance man. He was drafted in 1969 and served a tour of Vietnam. The experience changed him forever. He bounced across the country before settling in Miami where he found his calling managing construction and helping Veterans when he could.

---

[58] Flanders, Miami's Legion Park, 2003

Holcomb became post commander in 2010. Months into his tenure he got a phone call about a Veteran that needed help. He immediately jumped into action. Holcomb passed to his reward while riding a motorcycle he was helping move for that Veteran.

The post hosted *Operation Stand Down*, a weekend-long program developed to provide social services to homeless Veterans.

In time it seemed, the custom of showing respect to Veterans was no longer an imperative and their deeds were all but forgotten. [59]

In his address to the national convention, Commander Charles E. Schmidt said, "But look at all of the Guard and reserve units that have been activated since August 2, 1990. Look at the fact that the current membership window has been open for 27 years, by far the longest window in history of The American Legion. Instead of focusing on those deceased or ineligible veterans who cannot join The American Legion, let's put our efforts toward the more than 18 million who can."

---

[59] Stella Suberman, *The GI Bill Boys: A Memoir,* (Knoxville: University of Tennessee Press, 2012)

END OF AN ERA

Comrade Charles Frederick Adderley, a native of Miami's Overtown, was born March 3, 1924. The Adderley family emigrated from the Bahamas to Miami in 1910. He graduated from Booker T. Washington Jr./Sr High School. By the end of 1943, he was in the Army.

Adderley recalled landing on Normandy Beach in an interview with the Miami Herald: "As far as the eye could see there were ships all around us. Then there were explosions and casualties. Many, many casualties. It is an experience I can never forget."

In 2016 he was honored by France as a "Knight in the Legion of Honor," for his participation in World War II. His house was damaged by storms in the last few years. A number of charities came together and helped him rebuild and refurnish his home.

At the end of 2015, post leaders inked a deal with contractors to lease most of the post property to developers for 75 years. This lease would also include the building of a new post headquarters and a significant financial payment, which could finance the post in perpetuity.

A number of issues with the trust and questionable decisions within post leadership made the post's financial stability perilous.

2016 brought the post the ability to stand up a *Veteran's Wellness and Resource Center*, under the direction of Commander Robert Bellamy. It features talk-therapy and group counseling. Dozens of Veterans have taken advantage of the services.

The program is being studied for development at other posts.

In the Summer of 2017, after being unable to find a consistent meeting place or funding, Webelo Pack 29 dissolved.

2016 brought the demolition of post headquarters. Phot by author.

On Thanksgiving of 2017, Vice Commander Ric Love coordinated a giveaway of Thanksgiving turkeys for 25 needy National Guard Soldiers and families.

The Boys State program was reinvigorated and three young men were sponsored this year.

In January of 2018 the Americanism Committee re-established a relationship to provide continued support to Scouting in the entire South Florida region.

In support of Americanism, flags were donated to schools and a public park. A flag education program has been developed to send speakers to interested schools.

American sociologist Willard Waller said in his essay, *The Veteran Comes Back*:

> "From the point of view of the individual member, the contribution of the Veteran's organization is magical. By its alchemy, the organization transforms an experience that would otherwise be most destructive into a social asset. The ex-Soldier has lost his years, his youth, and he brings back the memory of nameless horrors. There is no place for him in civilian society. The Veteran's organization give him a place of honor. His fellow Soldiers understand him. They value his achievements.
>
> They do not tire of listening to him so long as he is willing to listen to them. When, like all heroes of the past, he is in danger of becoming a bore, the society of his fellows save him from this fate, so much worse than death."

As the first century of American Legion history comes to a close, Harvey W. Seeds has just over 240 active members.

We count among our membership, two WWII Veterans and only a handful of Korean War Veterans. The Vietnam generation is aging and the Persian Gulf and *War on Terror* Veterans have not joined in the numbers necessary to help the post thrive.

The organization is in constant danger of failing, but it has been in this position before and it has survived.

FOUR PILLARS

In 1919, The American Legion was founded on four pillars: Veterans Affairs & Rehabilitation, National Security, Americanism, and Children & Youth. Each of these pillars encompasses a variety of programs that benefit our nation's veterans, its service members, their families, the youth of America and ordinary citizens. These programs make a difference in hundreds of thousands of lives each year.

I. Veterans Affairs & Rehabilitation

- VA Claims Backlog
- Access to VA Health Care
- Network of Service Officers
- VA Vet Centers
- Health-care Funding Formula
- Veterans with Special Needs
- Volunteering
- Final Respects
- Heroes to Hometowns
- Careers for Veterans
- Homelessness
- GI Bill Benefits

II. National Security
- Support for the Troops
- Size of the Armed Forces
- Quality of Life
- Homeland Security
- POW/MIAs
- Operation Comfort Warriors

III. Americanism
- Flag Protection
- Illegal Immigration
- Voter Registration and Participation
- Boy Scouts of America
- The Pledge of Allegiance
- Establishment-Clause Lawsuits
- Legacy Run
- Boys Nation
- American Legion Baseball

IV. Children & Youth

- Child Pornography
- Catastrophic Illness
- Intellectual Disabilities
- Immunization
- Family Integrity
- Media Violence
- Drug Abuse
- Child Sexual Exploitation
- Family Support Network
- Temporary Financial Assistance
- Samsung Scholarship
- Child Welfare Foundation

HISTORICAL PROGRAMS

The history of Harvey W. Seeds Post #29 is a record of service to our community, our state and our nation.

With first-hand battlefield experience in what blood transfusions could do, the Veterans of Harvey Seeds stood at the forefront of organizing blood drives and in bolstering Miami's first blood bank.

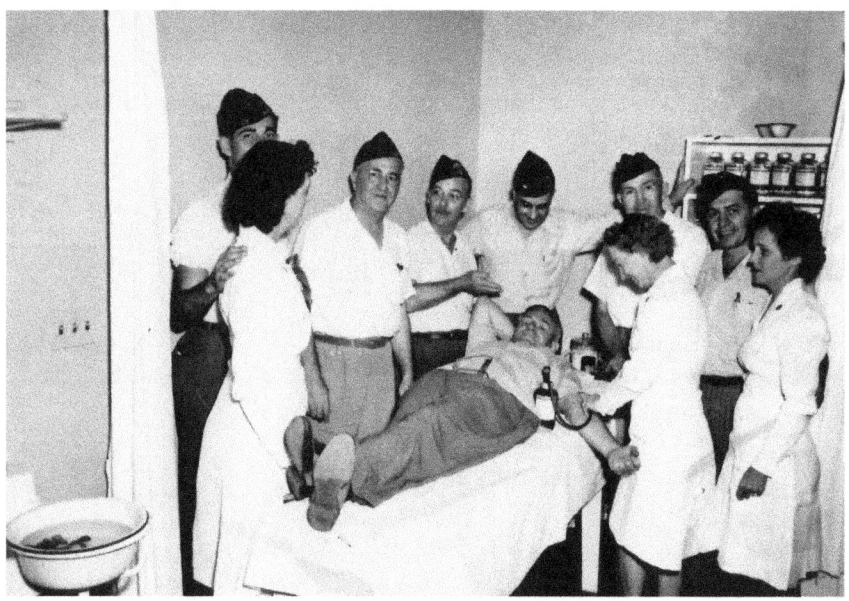

Blood donation was one of the tenets espoused early on within our post. Photo courtesy post archives.

Since 1919, American Legion posts have sponsored more than 2,500 Scouting units across the country. Annually, the Legion honors an Eagle Scout of the Year with a $10,000 scholarship.[60]

On Aug. 9, 1921, a Legion-led effort resulted in the creation of the U.S. Veterans Bureau, which later became the Veterans

---

[60] Legion, Legion.org, 2018

Administration.

In 1922 the national *40 & 8* began its child welfare programs starting a century of support for a myriad of worthy causes.

In 1924 the post funded a scholarship at the University of Florida for $300, a sizable sum at the time.

The post home was converted into a hospital and Red Cross shelter after the 1926 Great Miami Hurricane.

Approximately 20,000 young men annually participate in Boys State, a Legion program dedicated to promoting leadership. Boys State alumni include former President Bill Clinton, news commentator Tom Brokaw, professional basketball player Michael Jordan and astronaut Neil Armstrong.

Florida Boys State alumni include former Florida Governors Reuben Askew, Charlie Crist and Lawton Chiles.

Since 1938, The American Legion National High School Oratorical Program: "A Constitutional Speech Contest," has presented participants with an academic speaking challenge that teaches important leadership qualities, the history of our nation's laws, the ability to think and speak clearly, and an understanding of the duties, responsibilities, rights and privileges of American citizenship.

In 1939, as war loomed the post home on Biscayne and 64th became an official Red Cross Emergency Shelter.

During World War II, the American Legion and Auxiliary helped sell War Bonds.

In 1944, President Franklin D. Roosevelt signed into law the original GI Bill, or Servicemen's Readjustment Act, ushering in monumental changes in U.S. society. Six months earlier, The American Legion wrote the first draft of what later became the "GI Bill of Rights" – considered the Legion's single greatest legislative achievement. Higher education becomes democratized after 8 million veterans go to school on the GI Bill, get better jobs, buy houses in the suburbs and raise families.

The post joined the Miami Chamber of Commerce in multiple drives to eradicate Polio and other childhood diseases throughout the 1940's and 50's. The post sponsored one of the first iron lung machines to be brought to South Florida in hopes of giving therapy to Polio victims. By the end of 1952, over 55,000 Americans had been afflicted with Polio. Comrade and Past Commander AJ Cleary was integral in raising over $250,000 to find a cure for the disease.

In 1946 Miami Dade County hospitals were using just over 800 pints of blood a month for transfusions. Harvey Seeds was providing over 100 pints a month to the blood bank. The *Harvey W Seeds Blood Bank* was an innovative insurance arrangement by which people could donate for friends or family or could pre-pay a cash deposit in case they or someone who needed blood was injured or sick.

The post was so large in the late 40's that they were able to establish a 120-man strong Disaster Relief Committee which could respond to local emergencies. They were activated for at least three hurricanes.

In 1948 the post sent 32 boys to Boys State.

Realizing that up to 90% all Florida Highway Patrol were Veterans and or Legionnaires, in 1949 the post and the Department of

Florida petitioned the state to improve FHP pay and funding.

After the eradication of Polio, the post continued to support the research conducted by the *March of Dimes* to eradicate all childhood diseases.

In the 1950's and 60's, the post donated cash regularly to the Dade County Cancer Fund and the Miami Hearing Society.

As part of ongoing citizenship drives, the post helped, 'indoctrinate,' 918 new American citizens in 1952 alone. Citizenship Day became an annual event supported by the post and lasted well into the 1980's.

Throughout its history the *40 & 8* gave nursing scholarships to Jackson Memorial Hospital students. They also sponsored a "Milk Fund", where at numerous events, such as bridge tournaments they raised money for local schools.

The post supported Boy Scout Troop #329 in the 70's and 80's.

In the 1970's the post donated to the *Close-up Foundation*, a non-profit, non-partisan foundation that supported historical education.

The post has supported the National Commander's Foundation fund and the Florida Sheriff's Boys Ranch. Founded in 1957, the Florida Sherriff's Boys Ranch is a home for neglected, homeless and otherwise dependent boys.

The Legion donated $1 million to the Vietnam Veterans Memorial Fund for construction of the Wall in Washington, becoming the largest single contributor to the project.

Throughout its existence, the Legion has awarded medals and

certificates to outstanding boys and girls from elementary school through college. The award winners are usually cited for their courage, honor, leadership, patriotism, scholarship or service. A record of all award winners has never been compiled and is probably lost to time.

The American Legion provides free, professional assistance -- for any veteran -- in filing and pursuing benefits claims before the Department of Veterans Affairs through our Service Officers.

World War I Veteran's claims peaked in 1969. World War II claims peaked in 1986. The Vietnam Veteran claims, the Gulf War and War on Terror claims still increase year-over-year.

As Harvey W Seeds, Post #29 moves into its second century, post leadership has redoubled its commitment to expand the post's services to Veterans and the community through our *Wellness Center* and our dedication to each of the components of the *Four Pillars*.

PAST COMMANDERS & STAFF

1919-1920 Membership: 60
Commander: Robert Ralston (at right)
Board of Governors: E.K. Jaudon, Arthur G. Keene, Harry Sergeant, Guilford Green, William P Smith
Adjutant: J.T. Wigginton
Treasurer: H.G. Tuckerton

1920-1921
 Membership: 107
 Commanders: James M McCaskill, S.P. Robineau
Vice-Commander: Harry Acker
Secretaries: Dan Squires, A.F. Green
Historian: Arthur G. Keene

1921-1922 Membership: 210
Commander: A.J. Cleary
Vice-Commander: E.C. Allen
Adjutant: A.F. Given
Chaplain: Robert N Ward.
Historian: Arthur G. Keene

1922-1923 Membership: 304
Commander: Norris McElya
Vice-Commander: E.C. Allen
Adjutant: A.F. Given
Chaplain : Rev H.C. Gibson
Historian: Arthur G. Keene

1923-1924　　　　　　　　　　　　　Membership: 450
Commander: Charles A. Mills
Vice-Commanders: Earl Edholm,
Ralph C. Graham
Adjutants: A. F. Given, Welton A. Snow
Finance Officer: Lysle E. Fesler
Chaplain : Rev. Robert N. Ward
Historian: Arthur Keene

1924-1925　　　　　　　　　　　　Membership: 1101
Commander:　C. H. Reeder
Vice-Commanders: Lysle E. Fesler,
Joe Frank
Adjutant: Welton A. Snow,
Adelle M. Kendrick
Finance Officer:　O. A. Sandquist
Chaplain : Rev. Robert N. Ward
Historian: John F. Nolte

1925-1926　　　　　　　　　　　　Membership: 1595
Commander: Harry Goldstein (right)
Vice-Commanders: W. A. Snow,
L. E. Goodrich, Charles. P. Neider,
George La Vigne
Adjutant: Joe Frank
Finance Officer:　Lysle E. Fesler
Chaplain : Ben Axelroad
Historian: J. A. Cooper

1926-1927   Membership: 1695

Commander: R. V. Waters,
Vice-Commanders: Joe Frank,
Charles P. Neider, Leonard B. Spach, George La Vigne
Adjutant: John C. Norsk
Finance Officer: Lysle E. Fesler
Chaplain : R.N. Ward
Historian: Dan C. Squires

1927-1928   Membership: 1730

Commander: Virgil Ector (right)
Vice-Commanders: Leonard B. Spach,
F. J. Davenport, J. P. McDonough,
George M. Duncan
Adjutant: Joe Frank
Finance Officer: Lysle E. Fesler
Chaplain : Rev Frank A. Hamilton
Historian: Jack F. Nolte

1928-1929   Membership: 1012

Commander: L.E. Goodrich
Vice-Commanders: S. S. McCahill, Wm. McCarthy, H. U. Feibelman, Edmund Silverbrand
Adjutant: Joe Frank
Finance Officer: Lysle E. Fesler,
Chaplain : Rev W.V. Meredith
Historian: Jack F. Nolte

1929-1930 Membership: 850

Commander: Joe Frank (right)
Vice-Commanders: Roger Carter, F. J. Davenport, B.B. Freeland, H. U. Feibelman
Adjutant: John Norsk
Finance Officer: John Norsk
Chaplain : Ben Axelroad
Historian: Leonard T. Kendrick

1930-1931 Membership: 780

Commander: William Green
Vice-Commanders: Roger Carter, T. J. Kelly, Harry Acker, Wm. P. Davis,
Adjutant: H.D. Frain
Finance Officer: Vincent Grant
Chaplain : Edward Barker
Historian: Leonard T Kendrick

1931-1932 Membership: 887

Commander: Roger Carter
Vice-Commanders: William P. Davis, Thomas J. Kelly, Vic Strandel, Harry Acker
Adjutant: Harry Frain
Chaplain : Edwin Barker
Historian: W.H. Green

1932-1933   Membership: 661

Commander: William P Davis
V/C's: Harry Acker, Glen Mincer, A.C. Davis, Roy Schroder
Adjutant: Tim J. Browder
Finance Officer: William Green
Chaplain : Dr J.A. Camara
Historian: Fred Manning

1933-1934

Commander: Sam H. Roberts (right)
Vice-Commanders: Glen Mincer, M.M. Magner, John Bordas,
James Barney
Adjutant: Joe Frank
Finance Officer: Charles Cleveland
Historian: Fred Manning

1934-1935   Membership: 1027

Commander: Samuel S. McCahill
Vice-Commanders: M.M. Magner, John Bordas, James Barney, Harry Acker
Adjutant: Frank H. Cottrell
Finance Officer: Charles Cleveland
Historian: Fred Manning

1935-1936

Commander: Fred J. Manning
Vice-Commanders: L.T. McCarthy, Tim J . Browder, Harry Acker, M.M. Magner
Adjutant: Fred Meyer
Finance Officer: A.C. Davis
Historian: Fred J. Manning

1936-1937
Commander: John Bordas (right)
Vice-Commanders: Charles Grim, Claude Pullen, Norton Ganger,
J.P. Walker
Adjutant: Jerry Ganz
Finance Officer: Charles W. Cleveland
Chaplain : Edward Reedy
Historian: Fred H. Meyer

1937-1938 Membership: 783
Commander: Thomas J. Kelly
Vice-Commanders: Norton Ganger, Charles Sharman, Claude Pullen, J.K. Williams
Adjutant: Jerry Ganz
Finance Officer: Charles W. Cleveland
Chaplain : Edward N Reedy
Historian: Robert Lee Stephens

1938-1939
Commander: Thomas J. Kelly
Vice-Commanders: Norton Ganger, Charles Sharman, Claude Pullen,
J.K. Williams
Adjutant: Jerry Ganz
Finance Officer: Charles W. Cleveland
Chaplain : Glenn James
Historian: Robert Lee Stephens

1939-1940 Membership: 1234

Commander: James E. Barney
Vice-Commanders: Norton Ganger, William C. Brown, Charles Grimm, Arthur G. Keene
Adjutant: Jerry Ganz
Finance Officer: Charles W. Cleveland
Chaplain : Glenn James
Historian: Robert Lee Stephens

1940-1941 Membership: 1111

Commander: H. Frost Bailey (right)
Vice-Commanders: William C Brown, H.N. Fairbanks, F.R. Wickard, Arthur G. Keene
Adjutant: Jerry Ganz
Finance Officer: Charles W. Cleveland
Chaplain : Edward N Reedy
Historian: Robert Lee Stephens

1941-1942 Membership: 1275

Commander: John M. Murrell
Vice-Commanders: Norton R Ganger, Burt E. Bolton, Arthur G. Keene, Andrew G. O'Rourke
Adjutant: Jerry Ganz
Finance Officer: Charles W. Cleveland
Chaplain : Edward N Reedy
Historian: Herbert U. Feibelman

1942-1943 Membership: 1275
Commander: Norton R. Ganger
Vice-Commanders: Andrew G. O'Rourke, Herbert U. Feibelman, Lynn M. Shaw, I. A. J. Renno
Adjutant: Jerry Ganz, Lynn Shaw
Finance Officer: Frank L . MCMillan

1943-1944 Membership: 2048
Commander: Andrew W. O'Rourke (right)
Vice-Commanders: Lyle D. Holcomb, Lynn M. Shaw, Claude F. Pullen, John M. Deer
Adjutant: Jerry Ganz
Finance Officer: Frank L. McMillan
Chaplain : James Andrus
Historian: Herbert U. Feibelman

1944-1945 Membership: 3006
Commander: Lyle Holcomb
Vice-Commanders: A. E. Fuller, Lynn M. Shaw, J. Martin Deer, E. F Westfall
Adjutant: Jerry Ganz
Finance Officer: Frank L. McMillan
Historian: Herbert U. Feibelman

1945-1946 Membership: 6606
Commander: Lyle Holcomb
Vice-Commanders: J. Roe Driscoll, Wm R Simonds, Ralph B. Ferguson, Robert H Mayo
Adjutant: Jerry Ganz
Finance Officer: Frank L. McMillan
Historian: Herbert U. Feibelman

1946-1947 Membership: 6013

Commander: Martin J. Deer
Vice-Commanders: Walter H Brown, Thomas Q. Sharpe, Wm H Anthony, William R Simonds
Adjutant: Jerry Ganz
Finance Officer: Frank L. McMillan
Historian: Herbert U. Feibelman

1947-1948

Commander: Joe H. Adams (right)
Vice-Commanders: Walter H. Hanzo, Thomas Q. Sharpe, Hayes Wood, Frank T Imand
Adjutant: Jerry Ganz
Finance Officer: Frank L. McMillan
Historian: Herbert U. Feibelman

1948-1949 Membership: 5310

Commander: John McParland
Vice-Commanders: Ernest Allen, Sidney Crisp, Walter Hanzo, Thomas Q. Sharpe
Adjutant: Jerry Ganz
Finance Officer: Frank L. McMillan
Historian: Herbert U. Feibelman

1949-1950 Membership: 4741

Commander: Thomas J. Kelly
Vice-Commanders: Sidney Crisp, Roby Wetmore, James Griffin, Herbert W Noble
Adjutant: Jerry Ganz
Finance Officer: Frank L. McMillan
Chaplain : James H Andrus
Historian: Herbert U. Feibelman

1950-1951   Membership: 3986

Commander: Thomas J. Kelly (resigned) , Roby Wetmore
V.C's: Roby Wetmore, Ned M. Letts,
Fred C. Davant, Bernard Cooper
Adjutant: Jerry Ganz
Finance Officer: Howell G. Kase
Chaplain : James H Andrus
Historian: Herbert U. Feibelman

1951-1952   Membership: 3894

Commander: William J. Neale Jr. (right)
Vice-Commanders: Frank T. Imand, Mary W
Malone, Hugh J. Falvey, Thomas E. Lee
Adjutant: Jerry Ganz
Finance Officer: Howell J. Kase
Historian: Herbert U. Feibelman

A reunion of Past Commanders and Executive Committee members in the Trophy Room. Photo courtesy post archives.

1952-1953 Membership: 3754

Commander: Frank T. Imand
Vice-Commanders: James T Ross, William R Simonds, Pierce W Hopkins, Mary W Malone
Adjutant: Jerry Ganz
Finance Officer: Howell J. Kase
Chaplain : John M. Moyer
Historian: Herbert U. Feibelman

1953-1954 Membership: 2982

Commander: Thomas Q. Sharpe
VC's: William R Simonds, Robert L. Stewart, J. Emmett Grant, Edwin R. Greenfield
Adjutant: Jerry Ganz
Finance Officer: Cameron F Craig
Chaplain : Rev. Frank Titus
Historian: James B. Heath

1954-1955 Membership: 3049

Commander: Edwin R. Greenfield
VC's: James Ross, William Simonds, William H. Regan, James Akers
Adjutant: Jim Heath
Finance Officer: Lew Worrell
Chaplain : Frank Titus
Historian: Herbert Feibelman

1955-1956 Membership: 3049

Commander: James T. Ross
VC's: Joseph Friedman, Henry Halam, Fred Davant, William Regan
Finance Officer: Cameron F Craig
Chaplain : Elmer Weisbrod
Historian: Herbert Feibelman

1956-1957

Membership: 2957
Commander: Fred C. Davant (right)
Vice-Commanders: Robert J. Frick, Roy C. Jones, Robert Craig, C.J. Santucci
Adjutant: Joe Friedman
Finance Officer: Cameron F Craig
Chaplain: Elmer Weisbrod
Historian: Herbert Feibelman

1957-1958 Membership: 2904
Commander: Robert J. Frick
Vice-Commanders: C.J. Santucci, J. Emmett Grant, Roy C Jones, William C. Davis
Adjutant: Joe Friedman
Finance Officer: Cameron F Craig
Chaplain : Elmer Weisbrod
Historian: Herbert U. Feibelman

1958-1959
Membership: 3071
Commander: Henry J. Halam (right)
Vice-Commanders: George C. Smith, William E. Cox, Robert E. Craig, C.J. Santucci
Finance Officer: Cameron F. Craig
Chaplain : Elmer Weisbrod
Historian: Herbert U. Feibelman

1959-1960 Membership: 3101
Commander: J. K. Williams
Vice-Commanders: Andrew Burnell, C. J. Santucci, William E. Cox, Ron C. Jones
Finance Officer: Lawrence Woods
Chaplain : Elmer Weisbrod
Historian: Herbert U. Feibelman

1960-1961 Membership: 2965
Commander: George C. Smith
V.C's: Robert Craig, James Matthews, Kay S Thurston, Wm Davis
Adjutant: Joe Friedman
Finance Officer: John Ullrich
Chaplain : Elmer Weisbrod
Historian: Herbert U. Feibelman

1961-1962 Membership: 2919
Commander: Robert E. Craig
Finance Officer: Cameron F Craig
Historian: Claire V. DeConna

1962-1963 Membership: 2638
Commander: William S. Davis (right)
V.C's: Owen Bender, George Parkhurst, Homer Morrow, Joseph Catanzaro
Adjutant: William E. Cox
Finance Officer: Cameron F Craig
Chaplain : Elmer Weisbrod
Historian: Claire V. DeConna

1963-1964 Membership: 2664
Commander: Henry J. Halam
Finance Officer: Cameron F Craig
Adjutant: William E. Cox

1964-1965 Membership: 2665
Commander: Henry J. Halam
V.C's: Joseph M. Allen, William Rollins, William Sestito, David Blakeney
Adjutant: William Cox
Finance Officer: Cameron F Craig
Chaplain : Elmer Weisbrod
Historian: Albert R Cage

1965-1966   Membership: 2656

Commander: William E. Cox (right)
V.C's: Joseph Catanzaro, Joseph M. Allen, Thomas W. Hughes, Bill Sestito
Adjutant: Jack Hollander
Finance Officer: Cameron F. Craig
Chaplain : Albert R. Cage
Historian: Hortense M. Fotos

1966-1967   Membership: 2689

Commander: Robert E. Craig
V.C's: David Blakeney, Joseph Allen, Thomas W Hughes, Bill Sestito
Adjutant: Michael O Lewis
Finance Officer: Frank Meyer
Chaplain : Albert R. Cage
Historian: Hortense M. Fotos

1967-1968   Membership: 2827

Commander: David Blakeney
V.C's: Paul E Goodermuth, Joseph Allen, David Adelson, Hortense M. Fotos
Adjutant: Michael O Lewis
Finance Officer: Frank C Meyer
Chaplain : Albert Cage
Historian: Cameron F Craig

1968-1969 Membership: 2341
Commander: Joseph Catanzaro
V.C's: David Adelson, Andrew Fincham, Jacques Russell, Ernest R Dages , Stanley Sjostrom
Adjutant: Jack Adams
Finance Officer: Frank C. Meyer
Chaplain : Albert R. Cage
Historian: Henry F. Bronstein

1969-1970 Membership: 2912
Commander: Johnson E. Davis (right)
V.C's: Paul J O'Neill, William A Rollins, George Parkhurst, William Simonds
Finance Officer: Ernest R Dages
Chaplain : Albert R. Cage
Historian: Bette D Fairbrother

1970-1971
Membership:2830
Commander: David Adelson
V.C's: Paul E Goodermuth,, William A Rollins, William F Lynch, William E. Neumayer
Finance Officer: George E Howell
Chaplain : Albert R Cage
Historian: Barry T Sullivan

1971-1972 Membership:2663
Commander: Paul E Goodermuth
V.C's: Sidney W. Kirk, Dennis E Collins, William E. Neumayer, J.H.P von Hagen
Finance Officer: George E. Howell
Chaplain : Robert Birrell
Historian: Francis McGrath

1972-1973   Membership: 2588

Commander: William E. Neumayer
V.C's: Thomas Hughes, George E. Howell, Nicholas Williams
Chaplain: Robert Birrell
Historian: Francis McGrath

1973-1974   Membership: 2530

Commander: William J. Long
V.C's: Emile Fournier, Stanley Cann, William Dingiram, William Sestito
Finance Officer: George E. Howell
Chaplain : Robert Birrell
Historian: Frank C Meyer

1974-1975

Membership:2535
Commander: Stanley M. Cann (right)
V.C's: Thomas Hughes, William Rollins, Peter Jeffre, Charles Fidler
Adjutant: George E. Howell
Finance Officer: Randolph Spreen
Chaplain : Robert Birrell
Historian: Frank C Meyer

1975-1976   Membership: 2502

Commander: Robert Wheeler
V.C's: Thomas W. Hughes, William A. Rollins, Peter Joffre, Charles B. Fidler
Finance: Randolph E. Spreen
Chaplain : Robert Birrell
Historian: Frank C. Meyer

1976-1977 Membership: 2314
Commander: Randolph E. Spreen (right)
V.C's: Russell Hammerschmidt, James Wood, Joseph Oneto, Norman Naile
Adjutant: George E. Howell
Finance Officer: Bernice Bayne
Chaplain : Robert Birrell
Historian: Jim Henley (became V/C), Jim Wells

1977-1978 Membership: 2385
Commander: William J. Long
V.C's: James Henley, Jim Wood, Emile Fournier, Eugene Woods
Adjutant: Russ Hammerschmidt
Finance Officer: Francis McGrath
Chaplain : Robert Birrell
Historian: Georgia Lyons

1978-1979 Membership: 2010
Commander: Russ Hammerschmidt
V.C's: James Wood, William Rollins, Emile Fournier, Berniece Bayne
Adjutant: Norman Naile
Finance Officer: Edward Kelly
Chaplain : Robert Birrell
Historian: Doug McKenzie

1979-1980   Membership:2004

Commander: Eugene Woods
V.C's: Joe Catanzaro, Bill Rollins, Emile Fournier, Charles Old
Adjutant: Nick Williams
Finance Officer: James Catlett (asked to resign) Bernice Baynes
Chaplain : Bob Birrell (resigned) Brinkely
Historian: Russell Wilhite (resigned) J.H.P. Von Hagen

1980-1981   Membership:1741

Commander: Charles Old
V.C's: Francis McGrath, James Swan, Emile Fournier, Joe Marxer
Adjutant: Nick Williams
Finance Officer: Gene Woods
Chaplain : Lee Schroder
Historian: J.H.P. Von Hagen

1981-1982

Commander: Francis McGrath
V.C's: Donald Hedges, William Rollins, Dave Alston, Joseph Jamiel
Adjutant: Joe Elvena
Finance Officer: Eugene Woods
Chaplain : Claire De Conna
Historian: Joe Marxer

1982-1983

Commander: Charles Old
V.C's: Jim Swan, Don Hedges
Adjutant: Joe Elvena
Finance Officer: Ed Underwood (resigned)
Chaplain : Claire De Conna
Historian: Joe Marxer

1983-1984

Commander: Charles Old
V.C's: Bill Rollins, Jim Swan
Adjutant: Joe Elvena
Finance Officer: Nick Williams
Chaplain : Bud Kundquist
Historian: Joe Marxer

1984-1985

Commander: William (Bill) Sestito   (right)
V.C's: Earle Loomis, Jim Swan,
Adjutant: Joe Elvena
Finance Officer: Anna (Nan) Wolff
Chaplain : Joe Jamiel
Historian: Joe Marxer

1985-1986

Commander: Gordon Fenwick, Bill Sestito
V.C's: Bill Rollins, Jim Swan
Adjutant: Charles Old
Finance Officer: Anna (Nan) Wolff
Chaplain : Earle Lomis
Historian: Tony Barriga

1986-1987

Commander: Joe Elvena
V.C's: Ben Rogala, Bill Rollins
Adjutant: Charles Old
Finance Officer: Joe Marxer
Chaplain : Earle Loomis
Historian: Leo Abreu

1987-1988 Membership: 939

Commander: Jerry Speiser
V.C's: Jim Swan, Bill Rollins
Adjutant: Charles Old
Finance Officer: Jim Montgomery
Chaplain : Earle Loomis
Historian: Leo Abreu

1988-1989 Membership:1220

Commander: Joseph Elvena
V.C's: Dave Adams (resigned), Bill Sestito, Joe Marxer
Adjutant: Charles Old
Finance Officer: Jim Montgomery
Chaplain : Earle Loomis
Historian: A.J. Nicosia

1989-1990 Membership:1152

Commander: John Berryman
V.C's: Joe Marxer, Bill Rollins
Adjutant: Anna Wolff
Finance Officer: Jim Montgomery (resigned), Ed Kelly
Chaplain : Edward Loomis
Historian: Victor Rojas

1990-1991

Membership:982
Commander: John Berryman (resigned), James Swan (right)
V.C's: James Swan, Bill Sestito
Adjutant: Anna Wolff
Chaplain : Edward Loomis
Historian: Victor Rojas

1991-1992
Commander: Anna Wolff

1992-1993
Commander: Anna Wolff

1993-1994
Commander: James Colson

1994-1995
Commander: James Colson   (right)

1995-1996
Commander: Nick Williams
V.C's: Alfred H Underwood , Charlie Jones
Adjutant: Charles Old
Finance Officer: Albert Grandinetti
Chaplain : Joe Jamiel
Historian: Burnham Neill

1996-1997
Commander: Alfred H Underwood
V.C's: Andrew Thomas, Charles Jones
Adjutant: Nick Williams
Finance Officer: Albert Grandinetti
Chaplain : Joe Jamiel
Historian: Doris Jones

1997-1998
Commander: Al Grandinetti
V.C's: Doris Jones, Charles Jones
Adjutant: Nick Williams
Finance Officer: Larry McGrath
Chaplain : Joe Jamiel
Historian: Burnham Neill

1998-1999
Commander: Nick Williams
V.C's: Alfred H Underwood, Doris Jones

1999-2000
Commander: Doris Jones (right)

2000-2001
Commander: Nick William
V.C's: Alfred H Underwood, Doris Jones

2001-2002
Commander: Larry McGrath
V.C's: Mike Weber, Dan Oelker

2002-2003
Commander: Larry McGrath
V.C's: Larry Schatz, Dwight Fields

2003-2004
Commander: Larry McGrath
 Finance Officer: Dwight Fields

2004-2005
Commander: Philip A Johnson (right)
Finance Officer: Alfred H Underwood

2005-2006
Commander: Philip A Johnson
V.C's: Alfred H Underwood

2006-2007
Commander: Philip A Johnson
V.C's: Alfred H Underwood
Finance Officer: Robert A Flanders

2007-2008
Commander: Philip A Johnson
V.C's: Marcel Robert
Adjutant: Ted Guevara
Finance Officer: Robert A Flanders
Chaplain : James Colsun
Historian: Abrom Douglas

2008-2009
Commander: Philip A Johnson
V.C's: Robert Holcomb

2009-2010
Commander: Phillip Johnson
V.C.: Robert Flanders

2010-2011
Commander: Robert Holcomb
Adjutant: Ted Guevara
Chaplain : James Colson

2011-2012
Commander: Roger Kidder, William Hoppner
Adjutant: Ted Guevara
Chaplain : James Colson

2012-2013
Commander: Jonathan Black
V.C's: Robert N White, Robert Bellamy
Finance Officer: Claude Remy

2013-2014
Commander: Jonathan Black
V.C's: Robert N White, Robert Bellamy
Finance Officer: Claude Remy

2014-2015
Commander: Jonathan Black
V.C's: Robert N White, Robert Bellamy
Finance Officer: Claude Remy

2015-2016
Commander: Jonathan Black
V.C's: Robert N White
Adjutant: Richard Milhomme
Finance Officer: Claude Remy

2016-2017
Commander: Robert Bellamy
Adjutant: Richard Milhomme
Chaplain : Sylvester Barnes
Historian: Ralph A. Morales

2017-2018   Membership: 245

Commander: Robert Bellamy
V.C's: Kenny Wimberly, Ric Love
Adjutant: Richard Milhomme
Chaplain : Sylvester Barnes
Historian: Ralph A. Morales

2018-2019   Membership: 250

Commander: Robert Bellamy
V.C's: Ralph A. Morales, Kenny Wimberly
Adjutant: Richard Milhomme
Sgt-at-Arms: Charles Green
Chaplain : Sylvester Barnes
Historian: Frank Kornegay

Membership numbers were gleaned from scrapbooks and existing post documents.

CENTENNIAL HISTORY

AUXILIARY

The part that the women of America took in the training and equipping of their sons, husbands, brothers and fathers is a record of devoted service unsurpassed in the annals of peace or war.

To the full limit of their ability the wives, mothers, sisters and daughters of America supported and encouraged by their hands and hearts their men in the camps and at the front. Their spirit was as high and fine, their patriotism was as sincere and exalted, their service was as complete and unselfish as were those of the men who answered their country's call. [61]

The one incentive of the Auxiliary, as described in a 1934 Miami Herald Legion Edition, was, "the success of the Legion." To that end, the ladies sold millions of poppies yearly.

As late as 1934, the Florida Department's Auxiliary maintained a

---

[61] V.S. Thompson, *History, National American Legion Auxiliary,*. Pittsburgh: Jackson-Remlinger Printing Co., 1926)

salaried position at the Veteran's Hospital at Lake City, supported by poppy sales. The Auxiliary dedicated itself to assisting the families of hospitalized service members and providing shelter food and clothing when needed. They provided for tens of thousands of Christmas gifts for hospitalized Veterans.

Upon the invitation of Past Commander Mills, fifteen women met for a meeting in 1923, during which Mills asked for their help in standing up a ladies auxiliary. By the time the group organized itself enough to submit a charter request to the Florida Department, they had 40 members.

Past Auxiliary Presidents:

1924 Mrs. R.V. Waters
1925 Mrs. Roger Carter
1926 Mrs. George Duncan
1927 Mrs. F. Davenport
1928 Mrs. Edward Barker
1929 Mrs. Catherine Nieder
1930 Mrs. H Christian
1931 Mrs. S.S. McCahill
1932 Mrs. Helen Gibson
1933 Mrs. M.H. Presley
1934 Mrs. Edward Humer
1935 Mrs. William Stine
1936 Mrs. Roy Goddard
1937 Mrs. Ned Govro
1938 Mrs. Edward Westfall
1939 Mrs. Edward Westfall
1940 Mrs. P. Robinson
1941 Mrs. F. Johnson
1942 Mrs. Ed Williams
1943 Mrs. Hazel Tallamy
1944 Mrs. Hazel Tallamy
1945 Mrs. George Copinus
1946 Mrs. Alval Gleason
1947 Mrs. Jack Jason
1948 Mrs. Irma Brown
1949 Mrs. Irma Brown
1950 Mrs. Ed Morgan
1951 Mrs. Joyce Froom
1952 Mrs. Mae Vernet
1953 Mrs. Frost Bailey
1954 Mrs. William Leaming
1955 Mrs. Park Morrow

1956 Mrs. E Wesibrod　　　1957 Mrs. Cameron Craig
1958 Mrs. Ed Tepper　　　1959 Mrs. Nick Biglin
1960 Mrs. Margo Roberts　　1961 Mrs. Eva Jones
1962 Mrs. Mollie Rollins　　1963 Mrs. Freda Greenfield
1964 Mrs. Lucille Collins　　1965 Eleanor McMartin
1966 Mrs. Grace Barnes　　1967 Mrs. Herb Squires
1968 Mrs. P Goodermuth　　1969 Mrs. Walter Frank
1970 Mrs. Jack Kearney　　1971 Mrs. Andy Fincham
1972 Mrs. Andy Fincham　　1973 Mrs. Lillian Hedges
1974 Mrs. Andy Fincham　　1975 Bernice Squires
1976 Kay Dupree　　　　　1977 Emma HammerSchmidt
1978 Emma HammerSchmidt　1983 Maxine McGrath
1989 Kathy Marxer

The women of the auxiliary won the *Unit of Distinction* award for Florida in 1968 and a Meritorious Service award in 1973.

They probably earned dozens more accolades, however, those are lost to time.

40 & 8

"La Société des Quarante Hommes et Huit Chevaux," which is French, and translates as "The Society of Forty Men and Eight Horses," is an (now independent) honor society of American veterans, more commonly known as "The Forty & Eight".

They envisioned a new and different level of elite membership and camaraderie for leaders of the American Legion.

The title "40 & 8" comes from the box cars that were used to transport troops to the front in France. Each car had the emblem 40/8 stenciled on the sides, which meant that it could carry 40 men or 8 horses.

E.J. Reese applied for the charter of Voiture 492 on January 27, 1923.

Charter members were E.J. Reese, W.F.Perry, R.C. Graham, A.F. Given, C.A. Mills, H Kennison L Sperry, H.C. Schmidt, F.E. Davis, Walter Frank, John Bordas, Lysle Fesler, Sam Barco, Harry Acker ,W.A. Brock, Vistor Strand, W.W. Thompson, Arthur G Keene, W.L. Stine, M. Campbell and A.J. Cleary.

La Société has national programs that focus on child welfare, nurse's training, youth sports and the fight against Leprosy.

In October 1960 the Legion took a stand and told the 40 & 8 that if they remained segregated they would not be part of the greater organization. The 40 & 8 didn't budge. They created a new logo and maintained their Jim Crow ways.

Their web site states, "Our purpose is to uphold and defend the United States Constitution of the United States, to promote the well-being of veterans, their widows, widowers, and orphans, and to actively participate in selected charitable endeavors, which include among others, programs that promote child welfare and nurses training.

Membership is by invitation, and open only to honorably discharged veterans and honorably serving members of the United States Armed Forces.

During its existence, Voiture 492 focused on child welfare and nurse's training.

BASEBALL

"The idea to sponsor a summer league for 15 to 18-year-olds was first proposed by the Mill Bank, S.D., post in 1925. The concept was approved at the national convention. The following year, 16 states started Legion baseball leagues.

By 1938, more than 3,000 radio stations were broadcasting games.

Legion baseball earned a nationwide reputation. Only the best high school and junior college players under the age of 20 made the teams. It was an honor.

The 1935 Harvey Seeds baseball team won the Dade and Broward County districts and later lost to Post 12, West Palm Beach for the district championship.

Undated team photo. Courtesy post archives.

In 1942, as the World War II draft began scooping up all military-aged males, professional baseball players like Yogi Berra and Jack Maguire, Legion players began filling the void. St Louis' Stockholm post had eight members drafted from the Legion league to the major league in 1942-1943.

The 1948 World Series between the Cleveland Indians and Boston Braves boasted 31 former Legion players on both teams.

Miami hosted the 1953 American Legion World Series. Yakima, Washington Post 36 won.

The Pan Am Airlines World Airways, post 140 sponsored 1960's Region-3 winning team.

The Harvey Seeds team won the state's *Firecracker Tournament* on July 4th 1977.

Miami Post #346 won Region 3 in 1993 and won the World Series in 1994.

Undated team photo courtesy post archives.

In 2014 several post members attempted to support a baseball team, however, competing schedules and leagues have kept the number of interested players limited.

Major league stars like Bucky Dent, Steve Carlton and Charlie Hough once played on local Legion teams." [62]

According to the American Legion, as of 2018, there are 76 former American Legion baseball players in the Major League Baseball Hall of Fame.

---

[62] L. Robertson, *Is Sun setting on Legion baseball*. Miami Herald, (July 10, 1983) p. 14.

DRUM CORPS

1923 Harvey W. Seeds Drum and Bugle Corps, at their first competition, San Francisco. Photo courtesy post archives.

In the spring of 1923 a handful of Legionnaires, 18 to be exact, banded themselves together to form what was later to become one of the most widely known American Legion musical organizations in America, the Miami Drum and Bugle Corps of Harvey W. Seeds Post No. 29, The American legion, Miami, Florida.

Through the succeeding years, the Corps won the National Drum and Bugle Corps Championship in Paris, France, 1927; San Antonio Texas, 1928; Boston, Massachusetts, 1930 and Detroit Michigan, 1932.

Backed by a city, county, and state that appreciated the great publicity value of this organization, the Corps has attended all national Legion conventions since 1923 with the exception of Portland Oregon, in 1932 and the World War II years.

Only twice in these years has the Corps failed to compete in final. It holds the unique distinction of being the only Corps that has won a National Championship on foreign soil; in Paris, France and a State Championship in Havana, Cuba.

The Corps won its first State Championship in 1924 and has the official Department Drum Corps of the American legion for the State of Florida since that date, never having been defeated." [63]

Eleven members of the corps participated in all four national championships: Charles F. Curry, E.E. Edholm, Jerry Ganz, Harvey Howard, Kenneth James, M. M. Magner, R. A. Plastridge, I.J.A. Renno, H. C. Stansfield, J.R. Wardlaw, A.T. Wilkisson

"The corps uses a semi-military composition for its control. A Captain as its Chief Executive Officer, A First Lieutenant in each, its drum, bugle and color guard sections, Quartermaster in charge of uniforms and equipment..." [64]

After its second place showing in 1923, the group was hooked. The corps went back to Miami, raised funds, hired instructors and became better. They took 5th place in 1924 but failed to place in 1925.

Harvey W. Seeds Drum and Bugle Corps in Miami Beach circa 1927. Photo courtesy post archives.

---

[63] Jerry Ganz, *History. American Legion Conference Program*, 1958

[64] *Join a Drum Corps See The World*, Bugle and Drum Corps Times, 1949

Harvey W. Seeds Drum and Bugle Corps in at the Department convention, 1926. Photo courtesy post archives.

In 1926, the *Great Miami Hurricane* struck just weeks before the Philadelphia convention. The funds raised by the corps were turned over for hurricane relief. Corps members stopped practicing and helped Miami recover. The group didn't make the finals that year.

The next year, the corps joined 12 other corps in the now-legendary *Second AEF*. The Florida Commission of Agriculture donated over $28,000 for the unit to represent Florida in France. The 31 day tour covered all the battlefields of WWI where the corps performed for the president of France, King of Belgium and tens of thousands of Europeans during parades, memorials and an award-winning drum corps competition.

The Chamber of Commerce estimated that the drum corps produced over $7,000,000 worth of publicity for Miami in the 1927 season alone.

The media frenzy around the group was what one would equivocate with rock stars of later years.

The French Guard Republique band, pictured above, was twice the size of the Harvey W. Seeds Drum and Bugle Corps in 1927. Photo courtesy post archives.

In a bull fighting arena in San Antonio, Texas, the reigning world champions defended their title and won the 1928 title as well.

Shortly thereafter the City of Miami presented an orange flag to the drum corps in celebration of their multiple victories. The, 'banana-colored' flag was adopted by the Legion as the official championship flag and was subsequently awarded to champion drum corps.

The flag also had a corresponding trophy, the Russell G. Creviston trophy, named after a Past National Adjutant. The trophy is held at National Headquarters in Indianapolis.

After 1931, *The Great Depression* hit the corps hard. There was no money for instruments. There was no money for uniforms or travel. The corps did not attend the 1932 American Legion Convention.

The following year Florida held its Legion Department Convention in Havana. The post was able to obtain local and state funding support. The corps paraded through the streets, had a cultural exchange with the Cuban Police Band and won the state contest. At the national convention, they we are ahead going into the finals when they were disqualified on a technicality.

The Legion's national convention was in Miami for 1934. The drum corps was thwarted only because the rules at the time would not allow the unit to compete as the convention host city, however, the winning streak was at an end. The Harvey Seeds corps placed 3rd in 1941 and 1946 and won other state competitions, but never achieved another national championship.

The Third AEF in 1937 saw Harvey W. Seeds Drum and Bugle Corps in Europe just before war broke out.. Photo courtesy post archives.

Harvey Seeds' James S. Whitelaw was the National Championship rudimental drummer for 1935.

By the end of the war, 135 active Harvey Seeds drum corps members had been mobilized for World War II.

Undated corps cartoon. Courtesy post archives.

The 1943 Encyclopedia Britannica used a 1930 photo of Harvey W Seeds Drum and Bugle Corps as the definition of Drum and Bugle Corps.

By 1949 Harvey Seeds' drum corps had travelled over 162,000 miles, including two trips to Europe, two to Mexico, Canada and Cuba.

On different occasions the drum corps carried painted coconuts or crates of Florida oranges to cities they visited to promote the Sunshine State.

Drum corps had several membership posters. Poster courtesy archives.

After 20 years of limited successes, the corps took 1952 as a, "rebuild," year as some sports teams do. They changed their traditional style and modernized the drill and repertoire to keep up with marching trends. Many of the WWI veterans were out and the younger WWII Veterans had taken over. In 1953 and

1954 the drum corps travelled to Havana, Cuba for a Mardi Gras celebration and to Nassau, Bahamas for a parade.

That same year the National Executive Committee decreed that all national trophies would be held in perpetuity at the national headquarters museum.

American Legion support of drum corps activities was crucial to the activity's ability to thrive. Many of the forefathers of modern drum corps were drawn into the marching world as a result of their local American Legion or VFW post. You can draw a direct lineage between many Legion posts and corps in today's Drum Corps International (DCI) and Drum Corps Associates (DCA).

In 1955 the post sponsored the Miami Deputy Sherriff's Jr Drum Corps.

A September 5, 1961 *Miami Legionnaire* newsletter explains that the Harvey Seeds drum corps failed to attend the National Convention because their arrangement to fly with the 435th Troop Carrier Wing was usurped by the wing's activation for federal support of Korean military activities.

The *Harvey Seeds Rebels* sometimes carried a Confederate battle flag and wore civil war era caps, which was socially acceptable in those days.

Drum corps glory was not over for the post, however. Because of their successes, the group had sprouted a junior corps in the late 20's, which marched through the 1960's. The corps itself changed names, colors and musical styles in an effort to remain atop the marching arts field.

In 1957 corps members changed their name to the edgier and

more modern, *Miami Vanguard*, later reorganized as *The Vanguard* and finally *Legion of Brass* in 1971. By this time, a number of competing corps, such as the *Silhouettes*, based in North Miami Beach and funded by post #257, were stealing away members and staff,

Doug Crain's 1961 VFW National Individual Snare win and 7th place and Rudimental Quartet 12th place the same year brought great credit to the corps, which managed to hold on to musical greats like University of Miami percussion instructor and author, Vince Mott.

Several drum corps formed *Drum Corps Associates* in 1964, in an attempt to coordinate competitions and standardize them. Until that time each Legion Department would send the best corps in the state (as decided by one competition) to the national competition. Some corps kept their Legion sponsorships but many became independent.

Steve Vickers published *A History of Drum and Bugle Corps* in 2003. He noted that his two volume work was limited only by space and time. To that date he had knowledge of over 7000 drum and bugle corps that existed in the previous 80 years. He featured 86 of them in his publication. Harvey W. Seeds sponsored no fewer than 8 of the corps listed in Vickers' books.

After 1971 the senior corps split from the American Legion and went by the name *Florida Vanguard* and later *Florida Wave*. They left the American Legion and VFW corps circuits and began competing in a rival organization, Drum Corps International, DCI. That organization grew to overtake DCA as the premier marching drum corps competition platform.

Undated. Photo courtesy post archives.

COLOR GUARD

Color Guard competitions were born from the drum corps competitions.

The Glen R. Hillis Trophy is to be awarded annually to that color guard winning first prize in competition with all other color guards during the annual National Convention of The American Legion.

The Miami perpetual trophy, an orange flag, presented to the championship color guard each year, was established in 1929 and is the only Legion trophy given in the name of a city.

Harvey Seeds won National Championships in 1939 and 1941. They won many District and State championships throughout the years.

1941 National Champion Color Guard. Photo courtesy post archives.

GUARD OF HONOR

The first meeting of the Dade County Guard of Honor was at the end of 1938 at Coral Gables Post #98. Comrades Jerry Ganz and William Anthony proposed the organization after seeing the reception given to the remains of (Comrade Wallace H Smith) who was buried (at Arlington Cemetery) in Washington D.C. Ganz and Anthony brought the idea back to Florida.[65]

The group, however, not only conducted graveside services but they participated in the ceremonial installation of Legion post officers, they joined in the ceremonial portions of post openings, new member installations, patriotic holidays and any other events where they could perform as a color guard or rifle team.

For a number of years the Guard performed guard duty and occasionally brought in the colors at all the Orange Bowl football games.

The Guard of Honor was so highly regarded that Harvey Seeds and a number of other Legion posts agreed to donate a per-capita fixed amount, from membership dues, to support their activities.

---

[65] Feibelman, 1960

Dade County Guard of Honor, Photo courtesy post archives.

The Guard of Honor was composed of volunteers from different Legion posts. An accounting of the Guard's duties was not reported to our post, however, because many post members were in the Guard, a few documents and scrapbook postings survived.

From 1939 to 1959 the unit participated in at least 1500 funeral services. They were so well regarded that in 1946 the Captain of the unit, Al Lambert, was considered part of the post executive board.

In 1976 through 1977, one team logged over 1500 hours and 18,000 miles travelled in South Florida. Two members of the team had conducted 127 funeral services in a twelve month period.

In 2000 the National Defense Authorization Act provided for military honors for all eligible Veterans who wanted it. American Legion Post 98, Coral Gables, still provided full services for many Veterans as late as 2011.

Today the Army National Guard conducts about 85% of funeral services for the Army and about 20% of funeral services for the entire DOD. The rest are conducted by the active component, however Legion posts still maintain honor guards which they send to funerals whenever possible.

YOUR MEMBERSHIP CARD

The anecdote below was first found by this author in the 1977-1978 Harvey W Seeds Post History book. It was not attributed to another writer, so it can be assumed that it may be an original work by Historian Georgia Lyons.

Your membership card shows you belong to a great organization which, since 1919 has contributed so much to our country.

It is a small piece of paper, two and three-eighths by three and one-half inches in size. It is of no intrinsic value, it is not a bond, not a check, not a receipt for value. It is your Membership Card in the American Legion. It is a membership card in the greatest Veteran's organization in the world, The American Legion.

Your card tells you that you have entered into a material and spiritual kinship with your fellow Legionnaires; to practice the principles of freedom, justice and democracy; to care for the sick, the hungry, the needy and to be just to all mankind.

It tells you that no matter where you go in America, you are welcome to visit a place where good fellowship and comradeship prevail among Veterans and service-minded men and women.

Also, that when your final exit from this stage of life has been made, there will be gathered at your final rites, relatives, friends, comrades, and brothers who will recall to mind your virtues, though they may be few, and they will forget and forgive your faults.

POST #29 EVERLASTING

A number of Legionnaires not only served their country, but performed their civic duties in a greater capacity than was asked of them. With tens of thousands of men and women on the membership rolls, many have been omitted but here are a few of the firsts among equals:

Joe H. Adams: Past National Vice Commander (1951), Past Commander (1947), President Orange Bowl Committee, State Hotel Commissioner. Adams was pivotal in getting the American Legion to bring the 1948, 1951, 1955 and 1960 conventions to Miami. He was President of the Convention Corporations for three years. He was chairman of the county's Veteran's Service Center, Director of the State Chamber of Commerce and the Miami Dade County Chamber of Commerce, when not acting in a leadership role, Adams donated lamps, lighters and other needed supplies to Veterans recuperating in Miami's VA hospital.

H Frost Bailey: Past Department Commander (1946-1947) and Post Commander (1941). Bailey managed the organization during its wartime years, periods of great growth and tumult.

A.J. (Jack) Cleary: Known to thousands of Miamians as ," Mr. Polio,"Cleary devoted much of his adult life to funding Variety Children's Hospital and finding a cure for Infantile Paralysis, Polio. Cleary was chairman of the Miami Dade Blood Bank, an Elks trustee. He was the first president of the Hialeah Race Track. Cleary created the, "Empty Stocking Club," an organization that provided groceries for needy families. He helped feed thousands of families.

Johnson E Davis: Past Commander (1969), Past Department Commander (1971-1972), Past National Executive Committee Member

Herbert U. Feibelman: Past Post Historian, former President of the Miami branch of the Florida Bar Association and one of the founders of Temple Beth Israel, Comrade Feibelman was an avid historian and published a number of historical articles about varied subjects. He published two post histories (1949,1960) and was a trustee of Jackson Memorial Hospital.

Hortense Fotos: Yeomanette in the USNR in WWI, Fotos joined the post in 1964 and dove into every position imaginable. She was post Historian for two years and the department of Florida created an award for her because of her indefatigable work ethic. One year she logged over 520 hours of community service and was on at least seven committees. She was delegate to district and department conferences and volunteered at the USO.

Joe Frank: Past Department Commander (1944-1945), Past Commander (1929), VC (1926), Five-time Adjutant and multiple committee member. Frank was Captain of the championship drum corps in 1927. He is the model for the Marine at the Woodlawn monument. He assisted countless Veterans in claims while acting as Adjutant and Service Officer for the post.

Norton Ganger: Chairman of the State Veteran's Committee, Ganger was beloved by the drum corps for his twelve years of service to the organization. He was honorary captain of the corps and earned a gold life membership card from the post.

Jerry Ganz: Ganz was eulogized as, "The little man that did big jobs." He was pivotal in managing the Legion plot at Woodlawn Cemetery, as well as any project you put before him.

Harry Goldstein: Past Commander (1925) Goldstein was born in Antopol, Russia. He was drafted into the Quartermaster Corps in WWI but was never shipped overseas. Upon discharge he dedicated much of his time to Veteran's issues. He was a Miami Beach Commissioner for several years and spent countless hours on Veteran's issues, including keeping the books for the post for many years, for free.

Thomas J. Kelly: Past Commander (1937, 1938, 1949, 1950) Kelly grew up an orphan in New York. He was drafted into WWI as a Private and was wounded by Axis gas attacks as well as shrapnel. He went on to become a commander in the Coast Artillery and served state-side during WWII. Under his leadership and drill instruction the Harvey Seeds American Legion drum corps earned four national championships. Kelly was instrumental in securing the sale of part of the post property to the City of Miami and some would claim he saved the post by doing so. Kelly was the first commander to be elected multiple times. He was appointed Dade County Sheriff and resigned during his last tenure as Post Commander to take the position. When Kelly retired from the

Florida National Guard, he was promoted to the rank of Brigadier General.

Cesar La Monaca: A musical giant in Miami's history; La Monaca was born in Italy. He was playing a horn by age 7. He immigrated to America as a 14 year old unaccompanied minor and joined the famous *Banda Bianca* and later *Ellery's Italian Band* where he and his brother, Joseph made their mark in the music business. Joseph later went on to a music career with multiple symphonies.

La Monaca organized a number of bands across the country. He was drafted as an infantryman in WWI and later became the leader of the Army's camp band. He ran bands in California, New York, Rhode Island and the city of Hollywood in the 1920's. He mentored at least two Boy Scout drum corps and at least two other drum corps, including the Greater Miami Boys Drum and Bugle Corps. La Monaca penned at least three compositions to his adopted city of Miami; *Miami, Playground of the USA, March Bayfront Park and Strolling Along Bayfront Park. Playground* was named the official city song of Miami. La Monaca developed a 'French Horn Bugle,' which he never patented, but which was used by drum corps into the 1970's. Immediately after the Great Hurricane of 1926 he started a Bayfront concert series that lasted almost 50 years. He started the South Florida Youth Symphony. La Monaca joined the Florida National Guard in 1930 and served as Band Commander and Warrant Officer in the 265th Coast

Artillery Band until 1940. Under his musical tutelage the Harvey Seeds American Legion drum corps earned three national championships and countless other awards. La Monaca was lauded and loved by almost everyone he met and is considered by some to have been Miami's first great musical *Maestro*.

Samuel S. McCahill: Past Commander (1934), founding member of the post's *40 & 8* organization. He was a World War I Army Air Corps Major and a civilian attorney. McCahill provided the guidance the Legion needed during WWII as Florida's Department Commander and later two-term national executive committee member.

Charles Mills: Born Charles Muller to immigrant parents in New Jersey, Past Commander (1923) Mills and his entire family changed their name to show their patriotism when America went to war with Germany. Mills' family was considered Miami Pioneers as his father helped build the Royal Palm Hotel with Henry Flagler. He commissioned in the Navy before America joined in WWI. Immediately after the war he worked to keep and grow a U.S. naval station in Miami. He was a developer and hotelier by trade. He

worked extensively throughout his career to support Boy Scout activities and other philanthropic causes including the Red Cross. He served on the American Legion Florida Department executive committee. He was national Vice Commander of the American Legion. He was commander of the Military Order of the World War, an officer's group. He was Grand Chef de Gare and Grand Chef de Chemin de Fer of the 40 & 8.

Vincent Mott: Past Captain of the Harvey W Seeds American Legion Post #29 Drum Corps, professor of music at University of Miami and published author of a rudimental drumming instruction book still used today. Comrade Mott was Vice President of the National Association of Rudimental Drummers and an instructor of the Greater Miami Boys Drum and Bugle Corps. His influence as a teacher helped spread the art of percussion and drumming to future generations.

Robert Ralston: Every organization has its first leader. Ralston was ours. He and his brother were developers in and are responsible for Miami's first skyline, prior to 1926.

C.H. Reeder: Past Commander (1924) Reeder was City Auditor for four years before WWI. He was commissioned a lieutenant in WWI and was assigned to a railroad unit, as he had experience in that field. He was a City of Miami Commissioner and Mayor of Miami from 1929-1931 and again 1941-1943.

S.P. Robineau: Past Commander (1920) Simon Pierre Robineau was born in Versailles France. His father was a French surgeon who came to America to study combat surgery during the Civil War. Robineau became a pharmacist himself and helped develop one of the first commercial antiseptics, *Zonite*. He studied at the Sorbonne and later Harvard Law School before serving in the French army. He was wounded  in combat and taken as a POW until the US negotiated his release. When the US entered WWI, he commissioned as a 2nd Lieutenant in the Interpreter Corps and rose to the rank of Captain. In WWII, Robineau served as a Colonel for the Air Corps. His awards include the *Etoile Noire*, Purple Heart, Bronze Star, Legion of Merit and a citation from General 'Black Jack,' Pershing. Back at home he was a lawyer, investor and developer of the El Portal neighborhood. He was Miami's City Attorney from 1920-1922. He earned election to the Florida House of Representatives four times from 1929-1936 where he was known for having authored Florida's pari-mutuel betting laws and submitted the bill to change the state song to *Suwanee River* along with endorsing important legislation that supported the American Legion and all Veterans.

C.J. Santucci: Clarence (Sandy) Santucci joined the post in 1921. His 1968 resume listed Vice Commander, all Chairs, Baseball Committee, Boxing Chairman, VA Hospital and Children's Committee. He was best known, however, for managing Veteran's graves registration. Santucci was a constant advocate for a Veteran's cemetery in Florida and was beloved by his comrades.

W.P. Smith: A native of Live Oak, FL, William Pruden Smith was a veteran of WWI, serving as an engineer in the Florida State Guards. He became Mayor of Miami in November 1919 and organized the first meeting for Veterans of the war. He was a charter member of Harvey Seeds.

Junius Wigginton: Born in Paris, Kentucky, Wigginton was an Infantry Captain in the Florida National Guard. He served in France where he was wounded in combat. Wigginton was a charter member and the post's first department convention representative. He is the reason the post is named after Harvey W. Seeds.

Anna Wolff: A Navy WAVE after World War II, she worked in Washington D.C. in communications and intelligence. She became involved in the post after retiring in the 1980's. Anna, known as "Nan," served in a number of positions culminating in her becoming the first female post commander in 1991.

The roster of Harvey W. Seeds American Legion Post # 29 has been blessed with thousands of superlative men and women like those listed here.

CURRENT COMMANDER

Current commander, Robert Bellamy earned his membership in the American Legion through his service in the United States Navy. He served on the aircraft carrier, U.S.S. John F Kennedy (CV-67) and deployed to the Middle East during America's *War on Terror*.

He has completed two terms as Commander and has been able to stand up the post's *Wellness and Resource Center* for Veterans, his project to assist struggling Veterans with therapeutic and counseling needs, which is a model that other posts have found worthy of emulation.

WORKS CITED

American Legion HQ, *1927 American Legion Paris Convention*. Retrieved 04 23, 2017, from https://www.youtube.com/watch?v=dMhc7Xfu-iQ&t=755s

Associated Press, "Relief Expedition,". *Oshkosh Daily Northwestern*, (Sep 17, 1928). p. 21.

Atwood, Anthony, *A State of War: Florida from 1939 to 1945,* PhD Diss, (Miami, FIU, 2012)

British Movietone, *Attempted Assassination of President Roosevelt - 1933*. Retrieved 04 23, 2017, from https://www.youtube.com/watch?v=7EBxpnczKZk&feature=youtu.be

British Pathe, *Cermak Goes To Final Rest!* Retrieved 04 23, 2017, from https://www.youtube.com/watch?v=v2Lr-WDZcYA&feature=youtu.be

Bugle & Drum Corps Times Staff, " Join a Drum Corps See The World, "*The Bugle and Drum Corps Times*, (Oct 1949)

Critical Past, *The American Legion stages a parade...* Retrieved 04 23, 2017, from https://www.youtube.com/watch?v=lq5BdmVywM8&feature=youtu.be

Feibelman, H. U. *History of Harvey W . Seeds Post No. 29 American Legion* (Miami: Review Printing, 1960)

Flanders, Robert. *Miami's Legion Park*. Biscayne Boulevard Times, (2003)

Flanders, Robert, *American Legion Harvey W. Seeds Post #29. Biscayne Boulevard Times*, (Nov 2004)

Ganz, Jerry, *American Legion Conference Program*, 69. (1958)

Gray, Richard, *National Weather Service Weather Forecast Office.* Retrieved 09 24, 2016, from National Weather Service Weather Forecast Office: http://www.srh.noaa.gov/mfl/?n=miami_hurricane

Harold, Claudrena, N, *The Rise and Fall of the Garvey Movement in the Urban South, 1918–1942*. (New York, Routledge,2007)

History, *United States Army in the World War 1917-1919*. Retrieved 10 10, 2016, from Center of Military History: http://www.history.army.mil/html/books/023/23-6/CMH_Pub_23-6.pdf

James, Marquis, *A History of the American Legion*. (New York, William Green, 1923)

Keene, Arthur, G., Introduction-History Harvey W Seeds. In H. U. Feibelman, *History of Harvey W Seeds* (p. 37A), (Miami: Review Printing, 1960)

Kendrick, Leonard, T, "Harvey W Seeds Post is Oldest in Florida." *The Herald*, (Miami) 1930, September 28, p32.

Legion, American. (1943, October). *The National Legionnaire*. Retrieved 01 24, 2017, from The National Legionnaire: http://archive.legion.org/bitstream/handle/123456789/5828/aa002311.pdf

Legion, American. (1945, December). *The National Legionnaire*.

Retrieved 01 24, 2017, from The National Legionnaire: http://archive.legion.org/bitstream/handle/123456789/5857/aa002337.pdf

Legion, American. (1961, June). *American Legion Magazine*.

Legion, American, (2018, 02 18). *Legion.org*. Retrieved 02 18, 2018, from https://www.legion.org

Legion Wire Service, "Legion's Boys' Forum President Now Private, "*Legion Wire Service* (1947)

Legionnaire Staff. (1949, March 15). Lets Klose the Klan. *The Miami Legionnaire*, p. 4.

Lorini, Alessandra, "Convention Parade of the U.N.I.A.,", Negro World, 1 August 1921, GP: III, 566-68

Lukas, J. Anthony, "Report from Convention City." *NY Times*. (1972, July).

Lyons, Georgia, *Harvey Seeds History Scrapbook*. Miami. (1978)

Miami Herald Staff, "More than 1000 take part in Miami parade; Honor Seeds memory." *The Miami Herald*, (Oct 13, 1923). p. 1.

Miami Herald Staff, "Miami gains much by Legion's drum corps. " *The Herald*, (Oct 16, 1927), p. 32.

Miami Herald Staff,"American Legion Busy," *Miami Herald*, (Sep 29, 1926). p. 4.

Miami Herald Staff, "Armistice Speaker Assails Communism," *Miami Herald*, (Nov 12, 1937), p. 4A.

Miami Herald Staff Staff, "Asks Rum Curfew for Servicemen," *Miami Herald*, (June 28, 1942), p. 8A.

Miami Herald Staff, "Flashback Miami | The saga of Veteran's Village", (Jan. 27, 2016). Retrieved 05 08, 2017, from http://flashbackmiami.com/2016/01/27/veterans-village/

Moss, C.I. "2 Dade posts trying to recover history, " *Miami Herald*, (May 28, 1995) KE2

Pencak, William, *For God and Country,* (Boston: Northeastern University Press, 1989)

Robertson, Linda, "Is Sun setting on Legion baseball?", *Miami Herald*, (July 10, 1983). p. 14.

Rumer, Thomas A, *American Legion an Official History 1919-1989.* (New York, M. Evans and Company,1990)

Suberman, Stella, *The GI Bill Boys: A Memoir,* (Knoxville, University of Tennessee Press,2012)

Thompson, Vye, Smeigh, *History, National American Legion Auxiliary,* (Pittsburgh, Jackson-Remlinger Printing, 1926)

Wilbanks, William, *Forgotten Heroes: Police Officers Killed in Dade County, 1895-1995.* Paducah, (Kentucky, Turner Publishing Company, 1996)

Wilkinson, Jerry, *The Florida Keys Memorial*. Retrieved 02 12, 2018, from http://www.keyshistory.org/hurrmemorial.html

Williams, John, B., *History, Harvey W. Seeds Post No. 29*. Miami: American Legion. (1921)

INDEX

40 & 8 vi, viii, 34, 48, 90, 107, 113, 119, 143, 145, 176, 194, 200, 201

A.J. Cleary 43, 52, 147, 176

Adderley, Charles 136

Americanism iv, 68, 90, 99, 123, 125, 131, 137, 139, 140

Association of Veterans 23

Auxiliary vi, viii, 52, 69, 73, 80, 92, 98, 112, 128, 143, 173, 174,

Blood bank 97, 142, 144

Bonus Army 66, 68

Boy Scouts 33, 201, 203

Cermak, Anton 59, 60, 61, 20

Chamber of Commerce 22, 38, 47, 63, 144, 183, 196

Children & Youth 139, 141

Christian, William H. 54, 57, 78

Citizenship Day 102, 145

Cleary, AJ 98, 144, 196

Color Guard 50, 81, 191, 192

Craig, Cameron viii, 107, 174

Cuba 13, 15, 16, 53, 61, 72, 104, 105, 181, 186, 188

Depression 15, 46, 53, 59, 125, 183

Drum Corps 19, 24, 47, 53, 62, 93, 130, 181, 182, 183, 186, 188, 189, 198, 199, 200, 201, 202, 205

Feibelman, Herbert U. viii, 153, 154, 155, 156, 157, 159, 197

Florida National Guard 13, 16, 22, 45, 56, 62, 83, 91, 130, 198, 199, 203

Florida State Guard 75

Florida Wave 190

Fotos, Hortense 120, 197

211

Four Pillars 139, 146

Ganz, Jerry 99, 152, 153, 154, 155, 156, 157, 158, 182, 192, 198

Great Miami Hurricane 14, 41, 46, 143, 182

Guard of Honor 71, 107, 192, 193

Gulf War 128

Jacobson, Douglas 82, 83

Jaudon, E.K. 18, 32, 147

Kelly, Thomas J 56, 58, 65, 74, 94, 95, 96, 97, 103, 150, 152, 155, 156, 164, 167, 198

Korea xi, 96, 111

Korean War xi, 97, 99, 100, 130, 133, 138

La Monaca, Cesar *ix, 47, 56, 62, 130, 199*

Miami Legionnaire 51, 58, 107, 120, 188, 207

Charles Mills 18, 33, 34, 38, 48, 78, 200

National Convention 31, 47, 98, 102, 125, 188, 190

Orange Bowl 62 192, 196

Robineau, Simon Pierre 18, 19, 44, 63, 147, 202

Sewell, E.G. 47, 65

Sons of the American Legion, viii, 104, 106

T House, (*Tee House*) 63, 64, 92, 98, 108, 109

Veterans Affairs 139, 146

Veterans Village 85, 86

Vietnam xi, xii, 103, 106, 107, 111, 112, 113, 114, 116, 119, 121, 122, 123, 129, 132, 134, 138, 145, 146

Von Hagen 117, 165

Wellness Center 146

Woodlawn Cemetery 29, 36, 53, 67, 198

World War I x, 14, 18, 22, 26, 31, 66, 75, 88, 93, 123, 146, 200

World War II 15, 19, 72, 75, 78, 85, 86, 89, 93, 96, 100, 104, 130, 136, 143, 146, 179, 181, 186,

www.ingramcontent.com/pod-product-compliance
Lightning Source LLC
Chambersburg PA
CBHW050902160426
43194CB00011B/2260